D0671494

The Meaning of Life in Movies

Books by Michael Lister

Power in the Blood
Blood of the Lamb
Flesh and Blood
North Florida Noir
Double Exposure
Thunder Beach
Florida Heat Wave
The Body and the Blood
The Big Goodbye
Finding the Way Again
The Meaning of Life in Movies
Living in the Hot Now
Blood Sacrifice
Burnt Offerings
Separation Anxiety

For Judith,
Enjoy the show!
Best wishes
B Blessy!

The Meaning of Life in Movies

Michael Lister

2-8-12

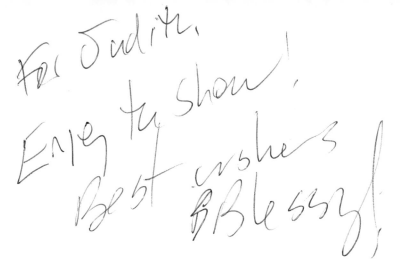

Pulpwood Press

You buy a book. We plant a tree.

Copyright © 2012 by Michael Lister

All rights reserved. No part of this book may be reproduced in any form or by any means, electronic or mechanical, including photocopying, recording, or by any information storage and retrieval system, without permission in writing from the publisher.

Inquiries should be addressed to:
Pulpwood Press
P.O. Box 35038
Panama City, FL 32412

Lister, Michael.
The Meaning of Life in Movies / Michael
Lister.
-----1st ed.
p.   cm.
ISBN: 978-1-888146-86-8 (hardback)
ISBN: 978-1-888146-87-5 (trade paperback)
ISBN: 978-1-888146-88-2 (ebook)

Library of Congress Control Number:

Book Design by Adam Ake

Printed in the United States

1 3 5 7 9 10 8 6 4 2

First Edition

For Dave Lloyd

Special thanks to Jill Mueller, Adam Ake, Jan Waddy, David Vest, Will Glover, and Jim Pascoe

The Meaning of Life in Movies

I spend a lot of time meditating about the meaning of life, a lot of time pursuing a life full of meaning, and lately, I've been thinking a lot about meaning within movies.

It's one thing to say movies can be meaningful. It's quite another to say the meaning of life can be found in them.

Meaning is defined as what is intended to be, the import, purpose, or significance of something.

Movies not only reflect and explore purpose and significance, their very existence is because of them. Not only are certain films highly significant to me, but I find the fact that there *are* films to be most significant of all.

We tell stories—and have for as long as we've been human—as a search for, an exploration of, and a way to transmit meaning. This is as true of the 17,000-year-old Lascaux cave paintings as the most recent serious novel or film.

Is there a purpose to life, a plan? Why are we here? What does it all mean? Is there true significance to existence or is it merely the result of random chaos momentarily materializing into something resembling order?

For me, the exploration of these ideas, the asking of the questions, is far more important than the conclusions reached. That we long for meaning is meaningful itself.

Film reflects life. In it, we see ourselves. Through it, through our identification with characters who become our surrogates, we have questions about life and meaning and significance and purpose asked and answered in a variety of ways.

Movies teach us that meaning can come from many places—there's not just one way to have a meaningful life. They teach us about the power of having a purpose, of being committed to something that transcends our small self-interests. As Rick Blaine in the act of sacrificing the great love of his life at the end of *Casablanca* says, "I'm no good at being noble, but it doesn't take much to see that the problems of three little people don't amount to a hill of beans in this crazy world."

They teach us of the inestimable value of friends, of people who care for us, and for whom we get to care. They show us just how absolutely essential love is for having a meaningful life. *Eternal Sunshine of the Spotless Mind* demonstrates the resilience and relentlessness of love, even as *Jack Goes Boating* and *Conversations with Other Women* speak to us of its fragility. Richard Curtis, in *Four Weddings and a Funeral, Notting Hill,* and *Love Actually*, reminds us again and again that love is not only what makes life worth living, but our imminent deaths bearable.

Perhaps more than anything else, movies remind us that the meaning of life is life itself. That we are here, now—alive, sentient beings, searching for meaning, struggling, hungering, failing, occasionally succeeding, is an awesome, awful, wonderful, wondrous, inspiring thing to behold and be a part of. Each of us is the protagonist of our own motion picture, the star (people made of exploding stars) of our own hero's journey. Our vision is unequal to the sweeping curve of life, of existence, and yet we occasionally catch a glimpse, perceive, however momentarily, just how meaningful the whole catastrophe of life really is.

And finally, films teach us of death, of the great loss none of us lose out on. I can think of no movie that does this any better than *Synecdoche, New York*. Everything we are, everything we know, everything that makes up our extraordinary and utterly idiosyncratic uniqueness will come to an end. As Roy, the more human than human-replicant in *Blade Runner*, says, "I've seen things you people wouldn't believe. Attack ships on fire off the shoulder of Orion. I watched C-beams glitter in the dark near the Tannhauser gate. All those moments will be lost in time, like tears in rain."

And yet...

We've lived. We've loved. We've been loved. We've lost. We've won. We've acted honorably. We've acted horribly. We've been, at moments, the best and worst versions of ourselves. And after everything, something of us still remains.

(This) Man's Search for Meaning

I'm a man on a mission—one that began very early in life.

I'm a seeker—searching far and wide—a traveler of inner and outer landscapes. There's nowhere I'm not willing to go, no journey too arduous, no climb too steep, no descent too deep.

After all these years, my desire is still at times overwhelming. I thirst with an unquenchable thirst, crave with an insatiable craving. I'm in pursuit of the thing I was pursued for—and though it can be called many things, it is one. What I'm after, what I've been looking for for so long, what I will ache for all my numbered days, is meaning.

From early adolescence, I have felt that life is fraught with meaning, and that to live a meaningful life requires a certain approach—mindfulness, openness, meditation, contemplation, abandon, deliberate study, intentional experience.

I find meaning in many places and through many experiences. My quest has led me to theology, philosophy, psychology, and to art. In fact, art is in and intertwined among everything—art in general and literature in particular. So much so, I can no longer distinguish between art and religion, art and philosophy, art and psychology, art and life.

Writing this book is a facet of my search for meaning. I'm looking for the meaning of life in every book I read, every movie and play I watch, every song I hear, every photograph and painting I gaze at. But reading and watching and gazing aren't enough. I also have to process, explore, contemplate—and that's where the book comes in. After all, how will I know what I think until I see what I write?

We live in a world where deep meaning (and therefore living) gets lost in shallow pursuits, in noise, in movement, in franticness and freneticness and forgetting what really matters most.

Viktor Frankl, Holocaust survivor and author of *Man's Search for Meaning,* observed, "Ever more people today have the means to live, but no meaning to live for."

Man's Search for Meaning chronicles Frankl's experiences as a Nazi concentration camp inmate and describes his psychotherapeutic method of finding a reason to live. If you haven't read it, I'd recommend not eating again until you do.

One of the main reasons I write novels (or columns or short stories or plays) is to have a more meaningful life. Through writing, I explore, I delve, I knead, I grope around in the dark searching for light. And I read for the same reason. Art is all about meaning—all about what it means to be human—to exist, to live, to love, to die.

I find art meaningful—both the creating of and the partaking of—as meaningful as anything in my life. That's why I spend the majority of my limited time on this pale blue dot making it and breathing it.

Many people spend time talking about and looking for *the* meaning of life—as if it's one thing to be discovered, a hidden ancient thing to uncover, but the meaning of life isn't one thing. It's many.

Frankl also said, "For the meaning of life differs from man to man, from day to day and from hour to hour. What matters, therefore, is not the meaning of life in general but rather the specific meaning of a person's life at a given moment."

Art works this way. I read a poem, get lost in a novel, go to see a film, pass a graffiti-covered boxcar or bridge, and all are messages from the universe—ethereal, ineffable, transcendent, true, all spoken to me in the present moment, the eternal now. I pause, breathe deeply, reflect, then continue moving again, only now with more meaning.

Giving ourselves over to art, letting it work its magic in us, is a way to have a meaningful life. Art speaks to the deepest part of our humanity. Artists create from the soul and the art they create speaks to our souls.

My quest for a meaningful life has led me time and again to art.

Art comforts. Art heals. Art teaches. Art inspires. Art transforms. Art broadens the mind and expands the soul and increases our compassion like very few things can.

Through art we can explore and experience the depraved depths and heroic heights of humanity—and be transformed in the process.

Frankl said, "Ultimately, man should not ask what the meaning of his life is, but rather he must recognize that it is he who is asked."

This very moment, you and I are being asked about the meaning of our lives. What will we answer? Art can tell us.

My wish for you is a deeply, profoundly meaningful life—and though there are a plethora of elements involved in such a thing, art needs be among them.

As both an artist and someone whose closest companions are art and artists, my faith is that of Joyce Carol Oates:

"I believe that art is the highest expression of the human spirit.

"I believe that we yearn to transcend the merely finite and ephemeral; to participate in something mysterious and communal called culture—and that this yearning is as strong in our species as the yearning to reproduce the species.

"Through the local or regional, through our individual voices, we work to create art that will speak to others who know nothing of us. In our very obliqueness to one another, an unexpected intimacy is born.

"The individual voice is the communal voice.

"The regional voice is the universal voice."

In the Beginning...

The end.

Beginnings and endings are not just causally, intimately, and irrevocably connected, they are one and the same.

As T.S. Elliot pointed out, "What we call the beginning is often the end. To make an end is to make a beginning. The end is where we start from."

Part of the reason beginnings are so messy, so chaotic, call for such strength and bravery, is that they involve the ending of something else. Perhaps the primary reason more people don't begin certain things is their unwillingness to end others. A new path requires us quitting an old one. A new life requires us ending our current one. A new relationship involves ending a previous one. To live, we must die. To find, we must lose. To have, we must give away.

Everything ends.

Everything begins too.

And, according to Mike Mills's masterful new movie *Beginners*, when it comes to relationships, we're all beginners.

Beginners imaginatively explores the hilarity, confusion, and surprises of love through the evolving consciousness of Oliver (Ewan McGregor). Oliver meets the irreverent and unpredictable Anna (Mélanie Laurent) only months after his father, Hal Fields (Academy

Award nominee Christopher Plummer), has passed away.

This new love floods Oliver with memories of his father, who, following the death of his wife of forty-five years, came out of the closet at age seventy-five to live a full, energized, and wonderfully tumultuous gay life—which included a younger boyfriend, Andy (Goran Visnjic). The upheavals of Hal's new honesty, by turns funny and moving, brought father and son closer than they'd ever been able to be. Now Oliver endeavors to love Anna with all the bravery, humor, and hope that his father taught him.

Beginners is by far the best movie I've seen in a very long time. The writing and directing are superb and the performances are sublime.

Deeply personal and profoundly universal, *Beginners* was inspired by Mike Mills's own father and is meant in turn to inspire everyone weighing their chances and choices in life and love.

Love is a choice we make, a way of being in the world, an approach to life, a worldview.

Every moment we are choosing life or death, love or fear.

At one point in the film, Anna says about romantic relationships that half the people don't think they ever work out, and the other half believe in magic. Like many of us, both Oliver and Anna want to believe in magic, but are finding it nearly impossible.

Why is believing in love, in the absolute magic of two lost souls finding one another and becoming one, so difficult? Why will some people never believe while others of us never stop believing?

Many people seem simply too afraid of the ending to make a beginning—and so let fear triumph over love. But magic happens when we choose love, decide to believe, dare to risk, when we surrender, when we trust and let love vanquish fear.

Even if nothing lasts forever (and I happen to be convinced love does), I'd rather be love's fool than fear's safe slave.

At seventy-five, Hal, Oliver's father, still believes. And he's the happier for it, his life richer, fuller, more meaningful.

Still, beginnings are hard.

Oliver and Anna are having an especially difficult time with theirs—with ending their lives apart and beginning their life together. Fortunately for them (and us), as John Heywood said, "A hard beginning maketh a good ending."

The end is in the beginning. Begin well and you will end well. It's up to you. Just ask Hal.

Make a beginning and ending today. Believe in magic. End fear and begin love. End your sentence in the self-imposed prison cell built of fear, guilt, cultural conventions, and the oppressive programming from wounded parents and wrongheaded religious leaders—and begin your paroled life in the brilliant light of unconditional acceptance.

When the Student Is Ready...

What is an education? How does one go about getting one? Where can both knowledge and wisdom be obtained? These are not only questions I've spent my life trying to answer, but those explored by the intelligent and insightful, smart and sexy new film, *An Education*.

In England in 1961, following a youth orchestra rehearsal, bright, beautiful schoolgirl Jenny is given a lift home by a charming older man, David. The two strike up a relationship that includes David's business partner, Danny, and Danny's vapid mistress, Helen. David charms and coaxes Jenny's protective parents into allowing him to take her to concerts, jazz clubs, and even to Paris.

David goes out of his way to show Jenny and her family that his interest in her is not improper and that he wants solely to expose her to cultural activities that she enjoys. Jenny quickly gets accustomed to the life David and his companions have shown her, and Jenny and David's relationship takes a romantic turn. After seeing Jenny dance with Danny, David hastily proposes marriage. Her father agrees to the engagement, and Jenny has to decide what kind of education she's going to pursue—David's lifestyle or higher education at Oxford.

Jenny's entire life is spent in pursuit of an education, but when she meets David, she realizes for the first time just how limited her, her parents', and her school's views of an education really are. What Jenny is experiencing and what she must confront reminds me of what John Adams said: "There are two educations. One should teach us how to make a living and the other how to live."

Life itself is an education—if we let it be. It's all in the approach—open, humble, hungry, or closed, stubborn, incurious.

Nothing troubles me more—not even greed or violence—than the vast segment of the world's population that is anti-intellectual and proudly, even militantly ignorant. Allan Bloom said that "education is the movement from darkness to light." Herein lies the great tragedy—light has come into the world, but people love darkness. We shouldn't be afraid of the unknown, but of the self-destructive defensiveness of not wanting to know. Wanting to know—asking, seeking, thinking—is the very beginning of education.

Education is any act or experience that has a formative effect on the mind, character, or physical ability of an individual, the process by which accumulated knowledge, skills, and values are deliberately transmitted and received.

Think about all those elements—*any* act or experience that has a formative effect on us, and the process by which accumulated knowledge is *deliberately* transmitted and received.

There are many, many ways to get an education. The vital thing is *that* we get one, not how we get it. And, of course, the best educations are those received through a variety of means, by a plethora of professors.

Are we being educated? If we're not, we only have ourselves to blame. We are responsible for our own education. And we have access to everything we ever need to receive the best education in the history of humanity—bookstores, libraries, museums, the internet, and life itself. When I think of all we have within our grasp and all the ways we fail to take advantage of it, I think of what Mark Twain said about reading: "The man who doesn't read good books has not advantage over the man who can't read them."

An Education is not merely entertaining, but inspirational. It's a wise and witty film, well made, well acted, well written. Nick Hornby wrote the screenplay based on British journalist Lynn Barber's autobiographical essay published in the literary magazine *Granta*. Barber's full memoir, *An Education*, was not published in book form until June 2009, when filming had already been completed.

This movie is magic—conveying so precisely, so powerfully

the longing for knowledge and experience by an open person ready for them, and the difficult choices involved in truly being educated.

Though *An Education* is filled with subtly brilliant performances—particularly by Rosamund Pike, Olivia Williams, and Peter Sarsgaard—Carey Mulligan's performance is absolutely sublime. Her Jenny is nearly equal parts old soul and silly school girl, worldly wise woman and naïve innocent child. For nearly my entire life, I've been mostly attracted to older women, but Mulligan's Jenny makes a compelling case against this practice.

Whether in her small bedroom alone with a book or on the streets of Paris, Jenny is hungry to learn, to breathe in every word, every sight, every sound, every experience. We have this in common. She thirsts, and the sheer power of it, its quintessential insatiability is overwhelming. I love this about Jenny, and it's this aspect of her I most identify with. These words are contained in all our other words; they are among the final words cried out by Jesus from the cross; they are the unspoken yearnings of mythic immortals who feed on the blood of others; they are the expression from the depths of every dry and dusty soul, barely hanging on in a parched wilderness wasteland—"I thirst."

Like Jenny, I've spent my life trying to "get my learn on." I started to say "my adult life," but my hunger for knowledge and true wisdom extends way back into childhood. It did, however, take a quantum leap when I finished my graduate degree and became a writer—which, after all, is how it's supposed to be. School in general and college in particular are meant to teach us how to think, how to educate ourselves. Henry Adams said, "They know enough who know how to learn."

In the midst of writing this, I happened to glance down at a bookshelf not far from my writing chair at two books I bought just for information—*An Incomplete Education* and *The Knowledge Book*. The books are two among thousands and thousands in my study/cave/sanctuary, for I truly believe what Thomas Carlyle said: "What we become depends on what we read after all of the professors have finished with us. The greatest university of all is a collection of books."

Buddhism teaches, "when the student is ready, the teacher will come." When Jenny was ready, David appeared. When we are ready, we will learn—which is why it's so important to continually remain in the humble posture of not-knowing, hungry, open, seeking. It's our best chance at a good education.

Stay open. Stay hungry. Stay ready. When we are, education will happen. We should be intentional about all things—but nothing more so than our education and enlightenment. Take. Eat. Original blessing comes from eating from the tree of knowledge *and* the tree of life. In fact, the tree of knowledge *is* the tree of life.

In the end, Jenny gets the best education—one that involves both heart and head, school and life, reading and experiencing. It's the kind of education I'm in daily pursuit of, and the one I most wish for you; the one that, if we all received it, would most change the world.

My Perfect Moonlight Movie

It occurred to me recently that I watch movies the way I read books—alone.

True, I don't watch every movie alone. Occasionally, I brave the theater and sometimes I even take a movie-watching companion, but mostly I watch movies in high-def on my Sony 55-inch HDTV in my study, reclined in my leather Stressless chair, surrounded by my books.

Not only do I watch movies alone, but I mostly watch them late at night when the world is sleeping—a trend that goes back to my adolescence as the only night owl in a house of early birds.

There's no better way to get caught up or swept away than alone with a good movie on the dark side of the witching hour. And some movies are just meant to be watched this way—*Frankie and Johnny* foremost among them. It's a movie about loneliness in which the crisis-ridden climax takes place on a long, lonely Saturday night as "Clair de Lune," which is French for moonlight, plays in the background.

Garry Marshall (*Pretty Woman*) directs the screen adaptation of Terence McNally's 1987 play *Frankie and Johnny in the Clair de Lune*, the story of an ex-con, short-order cook (Al Pacino) who drives a waitress (Michelle Pfeiffer) crazy with his intense courtship and professions of love. McNally adapted his two-character play for the screen and has expanded and rearranged his original story, adding a variety of settings and extending the narrative out over a longer period of time, while surrounding the lovers with additional characters. Kate Nelligan, another lonely waitress, and Nathan Lane, a gay neighbor, really stand out.

This exchange between Cora (Kate Nelligan), a waitress standing at the order counter trying to get the old, overweight cook, Tino, to finish her customer's food, is an example of the movie's good-humored humor:

> Cora: Tino! Who do ya gotta fuck to get a waffle around here?
> [Tino points at himself, Cora looks back at a customer]
> Cora: Forget the waffle!

Frankie and Johnny is a sweet story—but not overly so. There's a real sadness present too. These are people whose lives haven't turned out like they had hoped—for those among them with enough hope to even dare to hope. They are living lonely little lives of service and subsistence, but doing so with humor and dignity, and the desire to make real connections.

As charming and funny as *Frankie and Johnny* is, it's Al Pacino's and Michelle Pfeiffer's performances that elevate it—him, as a middle-aged man so desperate, he's needy and obnoxious; her, as a sad and wounded woman so gripped by fear she's hardened and defensive. Here are two examples of their typical interactions:

> Frankie: I feel like you're too needy.
> Johnny: Oh, come on. What does that mean?
> Frankie: I just feel like you want everything I am. You know?
> Johnny: Yes, I do. Why not?

> Frankie: I'm retired from dating.
> Johnny: What does that mean? Something happen to you as a kid? What happened?
> Frankie: You know, why is it that any time a woman doesn't want to get involved in a relationship, men think they were messed with as a kid? Wrong. They were messed with as a woman.

Each time I watch *Frankie and Johnny*, I feel the same way—connected, compassionate, happy, and hopeful. The movie is not without sadness and darkness, loss and lovelessness, but it's because, and not in spite, of these things that an earned sense of hope appears, grace out of the grime and grittiness.

In addition to the witty writing, charm, sweetness, and wonderful performances, *Frankie and Johnny* has a strong complimentary soundtrack—the best piece of music by far, "Clair de Lune," third movement of Suite bergamasque by Claude Debussy, a piano depiction of a Paul Verlaine poem.

When it begins to play on the small radio in her apartment, Frankie says, "That music is nice. Makes me think of grace."

I can't think of anything better than that, and as it turns out, it is a grace for Frankie and Johnny.

As Frankie once again begins to crawl back inside her distrust and defensiveness, Johnny calls the radio station's DJ and asks him to play it again in hopes it will save their relationship.

> Johnny: Now, there's a man and a woman. He's a cook. She's a waitress. Now, they meet and they don't connect. Only, she noticed him. He could feel it. And he noticed her. And they both knew it was going to happen. They made love, and for maybe one whole night, they forgot the ten million things that make people think, I don't love this person, I don't like this person, I don't know this—instead, it was perfect, and they were perfect. And that's all there was to know about. Only now, she's beginning to forget all that, and pretty soon he's going to forget it too.

Does he play it again? Does Frankie come out of her shell and risk love? Is it possible for two people to find later in life what was so excruciatingly elusive earlier, when they were younger and more hopeful and more sure?

Watch the movie or read the play, preferably alone and late at night, and let the "Clair de Lune" shine its grace on you, as you witness their story.

The Sacred Journey

I went to see *Eat, Pray, Love*, not because I expected it to be a great movie, but because its subject—namely how to live optimally—has been a lifelong pursuit of mine.

I'm so very grateful for the gift of my life, and sincerely attempt to put the most into it and get the most out of it. Toward that end, I continually ask myself the following questions (I'm not saying Liz Gilbert, the protagonist of *Eat, Pray, Love*, asks the same questions, just that her quest may have led her to some of the same answers):

 —Am I practicing love and kindness?

 —How do I obtain enlightenment?

 —What is the meaning of my life?

 —How do I truly savor every drop of juice from the sweet fruit of the tree of life?

 —Am I being mindful?

 —How awake am I? How aware? How alive?

 —Am I blindly following the culture I was born into or questioning everything in search of the truth?

 —Am I living justly and compassionately?

 —Am I making the world a better place by living unselfishly, extending myself for others, giving my gifts with joyous generosity?

I'm not saying I've figured out the best way to live—not even close—just that I've devoted myself to finding out the best way for me to live my life.

Liz Gilbert dedicated a year of her life to a similar pursuit. Here's how the studio describes the film:

> Liz Gilbert (Julia Roberts) had everything a modern woman is supposed to dream of having—a husband, a house, a successful career—yet like so many others, she found herself lost, confused, and searching for what she really wanted in life. Newly divorced and at a crossroads, Gilbert steps out of her comfort zone, risking everything to change her life, embarking on a journey around the world that becomes a quest for self-discovery. In her travels, she discovers the true pleasure of nourishment by eating in Italy; the power of prayer in India; and, finally and unexpectedly, the inner peace and balance of true love in Bali. Based upon the bestselling memoir by Elizabeth Gilbert, *Eat, Pray, Love* proves that there really is more than one way to let yourself go and see the world.

Eat, Pray, Love is better than I expected it to be, and, as usual, Julia Roberts is resplendent. The writing and directing are good—save for the way too much of the film is lit with a soft, ethereal quality from above and behind its actors, the overblown rim light putting a halo-like aura around Julia that I found extremely distracting (and it follows her no matter where she is—in a theater, a darkened room, even walking down an unlit street at night in Italy).

Liz's journey toward enlightenment, toward love, began because she'd lost her appetite for food and life and wanted to go someplace where she could marvel at something.

She's in crisis—recently divorced, floundering, trapped on a treadmill of meaningless, unintentional existence.

Like so many of us, it takes a crisis to move and motivate her. But we don't have to wait for crises to force us toward meaningful lives any more than we have to travel the world to find someplace to marvel at something.

Right now people from all over the world are traveling to Italy, India, and Bali attempting to eat, pray, and love their way to happiness and fulfillment, but the problem isn't our zip code. It's us.

Liz traveled around the world to find that the kingdom of God was within her all along. To walk the path, the way (of enlightenment, fulfillment, and love) doesn't require outward travel, but inward.

There's nothing wrong with travel, with an outward journey that symbolizes our inner one, but it's the smallest aspect, shortest distance, least important part of the true journey.

In the same way the best thing an education can do is to teach us how to be students for life, the best and only hope Liz has of a continuous life filled with meaningful eating, praying, and loving is if her journey caused her to be able to have the same experiences when she returned. If we can't find something to marvel at every single day, the problem isn't with the world or where we live, but with us and how we perceive.

And we don't have to devote ourselves to a guru to become our best selves. Or, if we do, it needn't be for long and we don't need to have just one. And no matter how helpful or inspiring or transformational we find certain leaders, we must inevitably shoot our gurus and sprinkle ashes on our Buddhas.

Like inspiration that becomes doctrine and eventually dogma, teachers, counselors, gurus too soon become gods, and our attachment to them ultimately leads to spiritual dependency and death.

Liz found what worked for her. You and I have to find what works for us. There are no rules. There is no one path, no one way to walk the Way.

Want to know the best approach to life? Ask anyone with a terminal disease. They'll tell you. Cast aside what really doesn't matter. Spend your few rare, precious, priceless moments on meaningful things of lasting value.

Liz tried new ways of living in an attempt to change her life— going to extremes and traveling the world. And it seems to have worked. But true, lasting change is about integration, about how we live every single day. It lasts because we're making lifestyle changes that lead us back to our best, most original selves. Diets don't work because they are faddish and temporary and don't constitute a true change in the way we live. The same is true of spiritual fads or programs or the latest, greatest teaching of the most popular guru or book or Oprah guest.

Lasting change is about integrating what really matters most into our lives.

Here's what I attempt (and fail) to do every day and what I recommend to you:

Be. Savor every second. Breathe deeply. Empty. Open heart and mind and belt to the wonderful, terrible, grace-filled catastrophe of life. Live with abandon. Love with passion and without reservation. Search for God—within and without. Be kind. Be still. Be silent. Be with supportive, nurturing friends. Be alone. Give. Give. Give. Ask. Seek. Knock. Sing. Dance. Make every meal a celebration. Make every day an adventure. Think. Create. Have lots of sex. Dream. Play. Protect the weak and vulnerable. Speak the truth. Fight for justice. Stand up for the oppressed. Be creative. To mine own individual, idiosyncratic self be true.

Only when these things become a way of life—something we live every day, not only on certain holy days or in certain exotic places—only when eating *is* praying and *everything* is love, will we be our best, deepest, most actualized selves and live our best, richest, most meaningful lives.

Romance and Rhetoric

The Russia House is a romance—of rhetoric as much as relationship, with ideas as much as individuals. It's about a scientist with the soul of a poet, a heroic drunk who finds it in himself to become a decent human being, and the bewitchingly beautiful woman who makes them both better men.

The Russia House, based on the John LeCarre novel, stars Sean Connery and Michelle Pfeiffer as two people caught in a web of spies and politics, whose love could prove fatal to them both. When Katya (Pfeiffer), a beautiful Russian book editor, attempts to send British publisher Barley Blair (Connery) a manuscript written by a noted Soviet scientist, she unwittingly draws them both into a world of international espionage. The manuscript, which contains information that could alter the balance of world power, is intercepted by the West's spy-masters, who then send Blair to Russia to gain more information on the mysterious document. But after Blair falls for Katya, he finds himself torn between his mission and the woman whose passion for her country and for Blair knows no bounds.

This is one of those rare films I return to time and again—twice a year on average—that continues to affect me deeply. I love its idealism. I love its romanticism. I love that it takes these two ways of being in the world and juxtaposes them with cynicism of the benighted, fearful men running the world.

The Russia House is a romance I can believe in, one that resonates with me, one that has credibility, one that is grounded in reality. It miraculously manages to be wise and profound about real issues of honor and justice, of love and hate, of life and death, yet remains wondrously, wildly romantic.

The events of *The Russia House* are set into motion because of these words by Barley at a writers' retreat in Russia during the Cold War:

> Barley : I believe in the new Russia. You may not, but
> I do. Years ago, it was just a pipe dream. Today, it's
> our only hope. We thought we could bankrupt you by
> raising the stakes in the arms race. Gambling with the
> fate of the human race.
> Russian writer: Barley, you won your gamble. Nuclear
> peace for years.
> Barley: Oh, rubbish. What peace? Ask the Czechs, the
> Vietnamese, the Koreans. Ask the Afghans. No. If there
> is to be hope, we must all betray our countries. We have
> to save each other, because all victims are equal. And
> none is more equal than others. It's everyone's duty to
> start the avalanche.
> Russian writer: A heroic thought, Barley.
> Barley: Listen, nowadays you have to think like a hero
> just to behave like a merely decent human being.

Later, a writer named Dante, who turns out to be a scientist as well as a poet, asks Barley to promise him that if he ever manages to act heroically, Barley will respond as a decent human being. Barley does, but when he discovers what Dante wants his help with, he wavers. Dante tells Barley that his thoughts on world peace have inspired him, which causes Barley to be confronted with whether he is willing to die for what he claims to be his most beloved beliefs.

> Barley : I'm not the man you thought I was.
> Dante: You do not have to remind me that man is not
> equal to his rhetoric.

None of us are equal to our rhetoric, but both Dante and

Barley manage to be when it really matters, making them decent and heroic, and reminding us that being brave isn't the absence of fear, but remaining resolute in spite of it. This, for me, makes *The Russia House* a profoundly inspiring film. If boozy Barley Blair can be a hero, so can I, so can you.

Sean Connery and Michelle Pfeiffer are absolutely brilliant in their roles as Barley and Katya, and though in general I hate the way Hollywood too often casts young women with old men, because of the characters and the casting, it works here. But as good as Connery is, Pfeiffer completely disappears into the role of Katya—something difficult for such an extremely beautiful woman to do. With her accent and mannerisms and the persona of the old Russian soul she's become, Pfeiffer *is* Katya.

The Russia House vividly and convincingly shows how few people—mostly scared, paranoid, small-souled men—keep the world from peace. It also shows the power of love.

Love, as the most powerful and powerless force in existence, gives us the inspiration and the ability to change, to become.

Love is the ultimate act of faith, of trust, and Cold War espionage provides a perfect backdrop of distrust to test the resolve of Dante, Barley, and Katya—lovers of truth, lovers of life, lovers of ideas, lovers of literature and art, lovers of people more than countries, of love and peace more than might and power.

Even in the face of certain death, Dante, Barley, and Katya hold fast to love, risking all for it—including their very lives—for they know what the author of the biblical book of the Song of Songs knew: "Set me as a seal upon your heart. For love is as strong as death."

Barley : I love you. All my failings were preparation
for meeting you. It's like nothing I have ever known.
It's unselfish love, grown-up love. You know it is. It's
mature, absolute, thrilling love.
Katya: I hope you are not being frivolous, Barley. My life
now only has room for truth.
Barley: You are my only country now.

Love conquers all. It changes us. It changes the world—toppling empires, removing regimes, lasting, remaining, enduring. Long after the Russian and American empires are ash-streaked heaps, love will still be changing hearts and minds, giving hope and strength, comforting, inspiring, transforming. Boozy Barley Blair acted heroically in the way only decent human beings can because of love. Love gently leads us to become our best selves, gives us the best hope of being equal to our romance and rhetoric. These three remain: faith, hope, and love, but the greatest of these is love.

Where Do Broken Hearts Go?

What do you do when your heart hurts?

As someone who attempts to live with a certain mindfulness, I try not to bypass a broken heart, try not to short-circuit the process no matter how painful, no matter how long. There's much to be gained from sitting with the saturnine experiences of existence.

I'm not advocating wallowing or prolonging or being miserable one moment more than we need be, just that there is benefit in the sad, in the sorrowful, in the song of the thorn birds fluttering around inside of us.

As Siddhartha so rightly stated, life is suffering. Pain is part of being a healthy human. I live, therefore I feel. And in addition to our own pain—that caused by others and the self-inflicted variety—there's the pain *of* others. Only the narcissistic feel only their own pain. Love, genuinely caring for an other, inevitably leads to pain. The more love we have, the more pain we have. He who loves ten has ten woes. He who loves fifty has fifty woes. The more capable of compassion we are, the more we will suffer. Compassion comes from two words that mean "to feel with." Feeling what others feel leads to additional pain and suffering.

Whether we choose to open ourselves to others and to their pain, or focus on ourselves and the thousand natural shocks that our flesh is heir to, pain, suffering, broken hearts are inevitable.

When my heart hurts, as it does right now, I think and feel, reflect and write, read and meditate, turning to art and religion for guidance and healing. Occasionally, I turn to trusted friends and counselors, but mostly I experience my sadness in solitude. And in my aloneness, few things comfort, console, and give care as much as the right movie.

It's true, books are better, but there's something so immediate about movies. Like fast-acting medicine, an old familiar film provides nearly instant relief.

I'm not recommending simple escapism, though there's certainly a place for that, but films that feel like old friends—available to us when old friends can't be and without all the guilt and calories that accompany comfort food.

I'm sure you have your own medicinal movies, but here are a few films that get me through you might try too.

No filmmaker makes me happier, cheers me up faster, than Richard Curtis. *Four Weddings and a Funeral*, *Notting Hill*, and *Love Actually* are movies I watch and quote from so repeatedly it seems as if I have them on a continual loop.

When I need inspiration, to be reminded of the difference one person can make, I pull *It's a Wonderful Life* and *Keys of the Kingdom* off my shelf—two films that, in numerous viewings, never fail to speak to something deep within me and make me cry like a little girl.

When I want to fall in love or be reminded of the possibilities of love—particularly for those whom it has seemed to pass by, I turn to *Before Sunset*, *Conversations with Other Women*, *Love Affair*, *Frankie and Johnny*, and *The Russia House*.

When I want to look at life from a different perspective, to see the world and love and relationships in a new way, Charlie Kaufman is what's called for, in particular, *Eternal Sunshine of the Spotless Mind* and *Synecdoche, New York*—movies that are moving, thought-provoking, awe-inspiring, devastating.

And for all the above—for love, romance, inspiration, sacrifice, making a difference, and just getting carried away—nothing the doctor orders can compare with *Casablanca*.

If my broken heart wants not to feel unbroken, but commiserate with other broken hearts, I find *Brief Encounter* and *The End of the Affair* particularly appealing.

Sometimes, when I'm laid low by life or love or something far more random, what I need is to just be swept away, to get caught up, or take off on an adventure. When I do, I return to *The Last of the Mohicans*, *Blade Runner*, *Spartan*, *Man on Fire*, *Déjà Vu*, *The Thomas Crown Affair*, *Nick and Nora's Infinite Playlist*, *The Holiday*, and *Dan in Real Life*.

And if I just need to laugh, nothing helps me quite as much as *Forgetting Sarah Marshall*, *The Hangover*, and, of course, a Richard Curtis film—most of which could go in all of these categories.

There are so many other movies I could mention. This list is not meant to be comprehensive. These are just where my broken heart goes, the ones I keep in my medicine cabinet—my first-aid kit for my in-case-of-emergency moments.

As you can see, among other things, I recommend movie therapy. Story gives meaning to our lives, and films provide a singular, immediate experience of story—art imitating life in narrative we can relate to and be inspired by. So the next time you're feeling broken, remember my prescription. Take two movies and call me in the morning.

Once Again and Again and Again

A man and a woman.

A mother and a father.

Divorced.

Having failed in relationships, trying again.

After dating a while, they're ready to have sex—or think they
are.

Nervous.

Scared.

Risking. Pressing through.

Then, suddenly, they go from awkward and uncomfortable to
her crying and him unable to continue.

Is it possible you might be who I need you to be? she asks.

It is. He is—and is not. And that's life—or at least a reflection
of it—art that is a recognizable reflection of human experiences more
than a few of us are likely to have.

It's a tender, true, affecting scene—one of many, not from a
feature film, but from a network television show.

There are actually "film" people who disdain television, as if
those who work in it—writers, directors, actors, producers—are less
somehow, as if the screen size isn't the only thing that's smaller. But
some of the very best-filmed fiction is made for television. Shows like

Buffy the Vampire Slayer, *Six Feet Under*, *Gilmore Girls*, *House*, *Mad Men*, and others are as good as anything on offer at the local movie theater—and these series are doing the equivalent of several feature-length films, season after season.

If it's true that TV is a writer's medium and film is a director's, it stands to reason that the best television has to offer will be richer, deeper, more intellectually and emotionally satisfying than all but the very best movies. Television allows for the time it takes to tell a complex tale while truly exploring the characters propelling it forward. It's why in general, novels adapt better to TV than film. It's also why so many accomplished and acclaimed writers, producers, actors, and even directors are drawn to television—particularly cable.

Recently, *Entertainment Weekly* listed what it deems as the five best divorce movies ever: *Kramer vs. Kramer*, *The Philadelphia Story*, *The War of the Roses*, *An Unmarried Woman*, and *The Odd Couple*. And maybe they are, but none of them delves as deeply or does so with such sustained exploration as does a too-early canceled TV show.

Divorce is death. A painful end to something at one point you never wanted to end—and maybe still don't. Failure. Rejection. Disappointment. Embarrassment.

Divorce is death, yet life continues. Not only your life, but that of your onetime spouse. Like an apparition, your ex haunts your life, a continual reminder of what was, of what might have been, of what is, of what can never be.

Divorce opens a family up and invites new people in. Lawyers. Counselors. Friends. Lovers. Strangers.

In the best of situations, divorce is difficult.

And this difficulty is handled deftly in the divorce drama *Once and Again*—one of the best adult hour-long dramas network television has ever produced.

Lily Manning (played by the breathtakingly beautiful and perfectly cast Sela Ward) is a fortyish suburban soccer mom living in Deerfield, Illinois. Recently separated from her philandering husband Jake (Jeffrey Nordling), Lily is raising her two daughters, insecure, anxiety-ridden fourteen-year-old Grace (Julia Whelan), and wide-eyed, innocent nine-year-old Zoe (Meredith Deane). For support, she turns to her more free-spirited younger sister, Judy (Marin Hinkle), with whom she works at their bookstore, called My Sister's Bookstore.

Lily's life changes when she meets Rick Sammler (Billy

Campbell) in the principal's office of Grace's school. Rick is a single father and co-head of an architectural firm, Sammler/Cassili Associates, which is located in downtown Chicago. Rick has been divorced from the rigid Karen (Susanna Thompson) for three years and has two children, Eli (Shane West), a sixteen-year-old basketball player with a learning disability, and sensitive twelve-year-old Jessie (Evan Rachel Wood), who longs for the days before her family's disintegration.

Lily and Rick share an immediate mutual attraction and begin dating. Their budding relationship causes problems in both of their respective families. Grace strongly objects to Lily and Rick's relationship as she still hopes to see her parents get back together. Karen, a public interest attorney at the downtown law firm of Harris, Riegert, and Sammler, is worried about the toll Rick's new relationship would take on their children, particularly Jessie, who is shy and emotionally fragile. She is also working through her own feelings of jealousy that Rick is in a new serious relationship.

Once and Again was created by Marshall Herskovitz and Edward Zwick, the same team behind *Thirtysomething*, and both shows demonstrate their brilliance for dramas that capture the nuance of entire epochs of modern American life.

Though the show begins with and centers around the romance and relationship between Lily and Rick, it also deals extensively with their children and to a lesser degree with their exes, Jake and Karen, and their ongoing struggles to find peace, joy, and love in the post-divorce environment.

Like *Thirtysomething*, *Once and Again* is smart, literate, well written, affecting, timely, timeless, and dramatic without too often being melodramatic.

It's also at times dizzily, intoxicatingly, wildly romantic. Rick and Lily have an earned and unexpected intensity and intimacy that combines the best of heady, youthful infatuation with the scars and wisdom age and experience and rejection and failure and the disappointment that divorce brings.

Few things are as therapeutic as talking. Few things need the healing therapy talk can bring as much as divorce. Each episode of *Once and Again*, as they're dealing with divorce and death and life and love and betrayal and fear and loss and hope, has the characters, shot in black and white, sit and talk—to us, the audience, making us their therapist, making us privy to their most hidden thoughts and feelings, making us more complicit in their lies and lives—and more compassionate. This makes TV more like a book—we know what characters are thinking, get to be in their heads, know what the other characters they are interacting with cannot.

In *Once and Again*, as in life, the past is prologue. Everything that comes around, comes around, not just once, but again. And again. Every seeming new issue in every seeming new relationship bares an amazing similarity to the issues and relationships that came before. We are products. We are patterns. We have dynamics, issues, wounds, experiences. We carry who we are into each new relationship, including what we've learned and lost, gained and changed, which makes the biggest part of our new relationships not new at all.

Divorce is difficult and dramatic and traumatic, and there's no one who hasn't been touched by its ripples. Fortunately, through story, we can learn and heal and grow and become more and better, and be our best selves even in brokenness, and, as far as divorce dramas go, *Once and Again* is a good place to start. Give it a try. You might watch it once. Or, like me, you might watch it again and again.

Rachel Getting Married Is a Home Movie Work of Art

I often drive eighty miles over to Tallahassee to see independent and foreign films at the Regal Miracle Five movie theater on Thomasville Road. Admittedly, eighty miles is a long way to travel for a movie, but the only time I've ever been disappointed was the one time I arrived to discover that the internet listing was wrong and the film I drove all that way to see wasn't there.

The times I actually got to watch the movie I drove over for—movies such as *Kiss Kiss, Bang Bang, November, Broken Flowers, You, Me, and Everyone We Know, The Lives of Others, Lonesome Jim*—I always thoroughly enjoyed them, and often left inspired.

Now, added to that list, is Jonathan Demme's *Rachel Getting Married.*

Though not as difficult to watch as *SherryBaby*, Demme's film certainly has its painful moments—watching awkward, addicted, in-denial people interact, particularly in the disturbing dynamic of dysfunctional families, can always make an audience uncomfortable.

Watching *Rachel Getting Married* is like stumbling upon the unfiltered, unedited outtakes of someone's home movies—deleted scenes that somehow didn't get deleted. We know we should look away, but quickly overtaken by the raw drama, we are unable to, so we stare, transfixed at the slow-motion wreck unfolding in front of us.

Demme's directing is stellar in his best film since *Silence of the Lambs*, and there are many fine performances, but this a breakout for Anne Hathaway, who takes full advantage of the amazing opportunity afforded her by the role of Kym.

When Kym (Hathaway) returns to the Buchman family home for the wedding of her sister Rachel (Rosemarie Dewitt), she brings a long history of personal crisis and family conflict along with her. The wedding party's abundant cast of friends and relations have gathered for an idyllic weekend of feasting, music, and love, but Kym, with her dark, tragic wit and knack for bombshell drama, is a catalyst for long-simmering tensions in the family dynamic.

Peopled with rich and eclectic characters, *Rachel Getting Married* is insightful, perceptive, provocative, profound, and occasionally hilarious. Director Demme, first-time writer Jenny Lumet, and the stellar cast lift this lean family drama into the best of these type movies.

Inspired by Dogme 95 films such as *The Celebration* and *The Idiot*, Demme shot *Rachel Getting Married* in HD video instead of film. His goal, "the most beautiful home movie ever made." He succeeds. *Rachel Getting Married* has the energy, spontaneity, and documentaryesque feel only video can achieve, but it also has the confidence, assurance, beauty, and performances only a skillful old filmmaker can achieve (this is Demme's thirty-sixth film).

Of all the reasons to recommend *Rachel Getting Married* to you, number one on the list is the profoundly painful performance by Anne Hathaway. Kym is not only her best role to date, it may just be the role of a lifetime, and, as if knowing that, Ms. Hathaway embodies the broken young woman to such an extent, she disappears into her.

Go see *Rachel Getting Married*—even if you have to drive eighty miles to do so. For as highly recommended as *Rachel Getting Married* is, the Regal Miracle Five is even more so.

Life Is but a Dream

Philip Seymour Hoffman's sweet, sad, sublime *Jack Goes Boating* is a small film about the biggest of things—things like love and loneliness and relationships and dreams and imagination and fear and betrayal and unforgiveness and life and death. It deals delicately with the beginning of one relationship and the deterioration and death of another.

Jack (Philip Seymour Hoffman—who also directs the film) and Connie (Amy Ryan) are two single people who on their own might continue to recede into the anonymous background of the city, but in each other begin to find the courage and desire to pursue their budding relationship. In contrast, the couple that introduced them, Clyde (John Ortiz) and Lucy (Daphne Rubin-Vega), are confronting unresolved issues in their marriage.

Jack is a limo driver with vague dreams of landing a job with the MTA and an obsession with reggae that has prompted him to begin a half-hearted attempt at growing dreadlocks. He spends most of his time hanging out with his best friend and fellow driver Clyde and Clyde's wife Lucy.

The couple set Jack up with Connie, Lucy's co-worker at a Brooklyn funeral home. Being with Connie inspires Jack to learn to cook, pursue a new career, and take swimming lessons from Clyde so he

can give Connie the romantic boat ride she dreams of. But as Jack and
Connie cautiously circle commitment, Clyde and Lucy's marriage begins
to disintegrate. From there, we watch as each couple comes face to face
with the inevitable path of their relationship.

The four characters who people *Jack Goes Boating* are isolated
icebergs, adrift, bumping into one another, the bulk of their beings
unseen, floating beneath the surface, each deeper and darker than they
appear.

Jack seems simple, even slow, but he is guileless and deliberate.
He, no less than Connie, Clyde, and Lucy, is wounded, suffering from
insult and injury, but most of all from isolation.

Jack and Connie, at the very beginning of their relationship,
bring into it the damage and baggage from their previous lives and
relationships. Clyde and Lucy have not only this, but the open wounds
they've inflicted on one another. Lucy tells Jack, "You've never been
in a relationship. A lot happens. Lot of good things. Lot of things you
wouldn't wish on your enemy." Lucy has hurt Clyde in ways she wouldn't
wish on her enemy, and though Clyde says he's worked through them,
there's real, deep-seated pain just beneath his mask of near constant
conviviality, just behind his kind eyes.

Perhaps more than anything else, *Jack Goes Boating* is about
dreams. Dreaming—actually imagining a different reality, is the
beginning of all things. *Jack Goes Boating* vividly and profoundly
demonstrates the connection between imagination and accomplishment,
between visualization and manifestation, and shows how closely and
intimately related to love they are.

On the shelf beside Connie's bed, half hidden by a picture
frame is a word carved from wooden letters affixed to a stand. Only
three letters of the word are visible, but I'm certain the word is *dream*.
It sits there next to where Connie dreams, where Jack and Connie lie as
they softly say what they're looking for in their "dream" partner.

Jack and Connie dream of lives different than the ones they
have—lives less lonely, lives lived in love with a loved one.

What is required for such lives? The desire, of course, then the
dream—the imagining, the visualizing—and then the leap, the choice
to live in love not fear, the action that enables love to conquer, then
vanquish, fear.

It all begins with the thing Einstein said was far more important
than intellect. Imagination.

In the myth of the Tower of Babel, when the Lord comes down and sees what the humans are up to—building a tower to heaven, building a civilization, making a name for themselves—the Lord says because of their imaginations nothing they dream up and set their collective minds and hands to will be impossible for them, and so confused their language so they couldn't understand each other. Like Jack, and the people in the story of the Tower of Babel, our greatest limitation is our imagination.

To accomplish what he does, Jack uses visualization—actually vividly imagining his actions before he takes them—something Hoffman, the director, uses to full affect.

Creative visualization refers to the practice of seeking to affect the outer world via changing our thoughts. It's the technique of using our imaginations to visualize specific behaviors or events occurring in our lives. The practice is a common spiritual exercise and is often used in sports psychology.

Connie wants to go boating. Jack wants to take her, but can't swim. Connie wants someone to cook for her, something she's never had. Jack wants to, but doesn't know how. Through love—love as an act of imagination, love as an action, love as both the dreaming and doing that conquers all fear—Jack becomes an excellent swimmer and cook, heroic in the way only the truest lovers can be.

Jack Goes Boating is witty and funny and charming and likable, but it's also, by turns, sad, even heartbreaking. Amy Ryan, as ever, is extraordinary. Philip Seymour Hoffman is, as usual, brilliant and beautiful, and in addition to being one of my favorite actors, doing the most interesting and profoundly moving work these days, he may also soon be one of my favorite directors. He's off to an amazing start. Go boating and swimming and cooking with Jack as soon as you can. Learn from his fearlessness. Be inspired by his love. And like him, visualize the life you want to have.

I drove over a hundred miles to go boating with Jack. The film is so good it'd be worth a trip ten times that. Maybe more. No, definitely more. Infinitely more.

Here. Now. After.

What happens when we die?

No one knows with any certainty, but that doesn't keep certain people from acting as if they do, from answering the question with conviction and certitude.

Is this it or is there more?

As I write this, as you read it, we are living beings on a small blue dot, who one day all too soon won't be. We are alive now. In a blink, we will be gone. This life—all we love, all that matters, all we value and cherish—will be lost. The question is, will everything be lost forever? Is there a beyond? If so, what of this life do we take into the next? "Ay, there's the rub. For in that sleep of death what dreams may come, When we have shuffled off this mortal coil, Must give us pause."

And a great pause it is. So necessary, so beneficial.

The specific reason for Hamlet's pause may not be good, but pause itself is.

Perhaps this pause is the greatest loss people who have fooled themselves into certitude suffer. It's the pause of not knowing, the humility that comes from doubt and openness and critical thinking. The greatest atrocities throughout human history have been committed by people with no pause—no doubt, no lack of faith, no uncertainty, no reflection.

I'm grateful for the pause, for the mystery, for the unknown, for the space to explore and question and reflect. This pause, this emptiness and openness comes not because there are general unknowns awaiting discovery, but because there are specific unknowables that are themselves the discovery.

Being alive. Knowing we're going to die. Not knowing anything else. The human condition lends itself to pause, to reflection, to hope, to speculation.

Is the afterlife merely an extension of this one—but in a spiritual realm? Is it radically different? Are there rewards and punishments as so many believe? Or is there nothing at all?

Clint Eastwood's new film *Hereafter* ostensibly deals with these questions.

Hereafter tells the story of three people who are touched by death in different ways. George is a blue-collar American who has a special connection to the afterlife. On the other side of the world, Marie, a French journalist, has a near-death experience that shakes her reality. And when Marcus, a London schoolboy, loses the person closest to him, he desperately needs answers. Each on a path in search of the truth, their lives will intersect, forever changed by what they believe might—or must—exist in the hereafter.

Hereafter continues Eastwood's late-in-life brilliant filmmaking (his butchering of Michael Connelly's *Blood Work* was his last lazy movie). It's a quietly affecting, if occasionally slow, character-study work of art. It's hopeful—as most things having to do with the afterlife are—and never hokey. It's beautiful, and the three main performances are truly inspired.

I hope this film finds its audience, but I'm doubtful. The trailer makes it look as if it's a thriller—or at least has some thriller elements. It is not. It does not. It's a drama, even a bit of a romance, and the three eventually intersecting stories unspool so leisurely, carefully, even slowly that they require a certain measure of patience.

More than the afterlife—as is always the case—the film is about the present life ("as below, so above; in heaven as on earth"). It's about three lonely people, who because of trauma, loss, and the burdens of an unwanted gift and unexpected knowledge find themselves isolated, adrift, open, searching.

In this, George's unwanted, burdensome gift of "sight," *Hereafter* reminds me of *The Gift*, a fine film starring Cate Blanchett, worth seeing if you haven't. In it, Cate's character Annie has a gift similar to George, and with it, a similar burden to bear. The two films can be viewed as different genre takes (one drama, one thriller) on a related theme. Insight, the ability to see what so many others cannot, causes George, and later Marie, to fail to fit in, which in a world where conformity is the greatest of virtues, is the greatest of sins. The things that make us extraordinary, different, diverse, interesting cause us to have something of benefit to offer, are the very things that cause fearful, insecure, conformists to shun and vilify us. That outsiders, "others," are not or do not have to be completely and utterly alone is the great hope the film offers—for this and the afterlife.

Hamlet's pause, the one that made him "rather bear the ills he knew than fly to others he knew not of," was caused by the "dread of something after death," but love (and the hope found in *Hereafter*) assures us we have nothing to fear either in this life or from "the undiscovered country from whose bourn no traveler returns." Fear kept Hamlet from killing himself, but not from self-destruction. Perfect love—the kind that casts out all fear, lets us live free, with a childlike abandon—trusts in this life, no less in what dreams may come.

The Obssesion of *Zodiac*

My friend Michael Connelly, one of the world's greatest practitioners of police procedurals, often says the best cases aren't the ones cops work on, but the ones that work on cops.

It's a profound statement—one that Connelly attributes to Joseph Heller (if memory serves)—and as I watched David Fincher's *Zodiac*, I kept thinking about it. Few cases worked on those who worked on it like the Zodiac killer case—and not just cops, but reporters, forensics experts, and even a cartoonist.

It's the stuff of enduring crime fiction—the unsolved case that clings to a cop like little bits of karma, haunting his or her work-obsessed days and sleepless, gin-soaked nights.

With respect to Brad and Benjamin, David Fincher's masterwork is not the curious case of the backwards growing man-boy, but the disquieting case of the letter-writing serial killer who called himself the Zodiac.

More police procedural than a slick serial-killer flick, *Zodiac* is a slow-burn of a crime film that creeps into your consciousness and just sits there, waiting, breathing, readying to strike. It follows the investigation of the Zodiac killings that terrorized the San Francisco Bay area in the late 60s and early 70s. The Zodiac not only killed people, but created a Jack the Ripper aura by sending letters to the newspapers and daring readers to solve coded messages. But the film's focus isn't on the Zodiac so much as those who are working on and being worked on by his case.

All the performances in *Zodiac* are outstanding. Even so, some stand out among them—the amazing Robert Downey Jr., the awkward hero/cartoonist, Jake Gyllenhaal, and the hard-working cop, Mark Ruffalo.

Fincher and his genius cinematographer Harris Savides capture the period and feel of the city with restraint and precision, and James Vanderbilt's screenplay is a throwback to character-driven storytelling far too rare these days.

The 70s are considered by many to be American cinema's best decade ever, so it's the highest compliment I can give this film and its director to say that it really fits well in the period in which it's set. Put *Zodiac* right alongside *Chinatown*, *The Godfather*, *The Exorcist*, and *The French Connection*. It holds up. Put the name Fincher right alongside auteurs Coppola, Polanski, and Scorsese. He holds his own.

More than anything else, I think *Zodiac* is about obsession. The cops and newspaper men's obsession with the Zodiac no less than David Fincher's obsession with filmmaking or Robert Downey Jr.'s obsession with acting. This is something I understand, and it reminds me of a quote by John Gardner I often think of when I'm suffering from the tunnel vision working on a novel brings. "True artists, whatever smiling face they may show you, are obsessive, driven people." People who are good at what they do are obsessed with it—this is no less true of teachers and homemakers than serial killers and cops.

Zodiac reminds me of a complex song. Unlike its pop counterparts, it's not as catchy or obviously infectious at first, but long after bubble gum pop has lost its flavor, a great song that had to grow on you endures. I've seen *Zodiac* some five or six times now, and it only gets better with subsequent viewings, which makes it truly remarkable—a perfect 70s-era character-driven police procedural.

The Precious Illusions of a Perfect Film

There's entertainment, then there's art.

Then there's art that entertains.

Alfred Hitchcock was a master—a genius with a rare talent that garnered him both commercial and critical success, a true artist who worked within the studio system and entertained the masses. His work includes some of the greatest, most extraordinary films ever made. But the master's masterpiece is unquestionably *Vertigo*.

I've lost track of how many times I've seen this extraordinary film (probably close to thirty times), but my most recent screening was in high definition thanks to Apple TV, and it was stunning.

I think a convincing case can be made that *Vertigo* is the greatest, most flawless film ever made, but even critics and scholars unwilling to go that far say it's in some very elite company.

Truth is, you can't go wrong with any Hitchcock flick, particularly those from the 40s and 50s, beginning with *Saboteur* and ending with *Marnie*. There are so many remarkable films from this period, including *Suspicion, Spellbound, Shadow of a Doubt, Notorious, Strangers on a Train, I Confess, Rear Window, North by Northwest, Psycho,* and *The Birds*.

Stop and think about it for a moment. Those are some of the

very best the art of cinema has to offer, and they were all made by this one amazing artist and the collaborators he assembled, but as amazing as all of Hitchcock's films are, *Vertigo* is singular, peerless, surpassing even his own astonishing achievements.

Based on the French novel *D'Entre Les Morts* (*From Among the Dead*) by Pierre Boileau and Thomas Narcejac, the script for *Vertigo* was written by Alec Coppel and Samuel Taylor, though like all his movies, Hitch's hand can be seen here, as well.

John "Scottie" Ferguson (Jimmy Stewart) is a retired San Francisco police detective who suffers from acrophobia and Madeleine (Kim Novak) is the lady who leads him to high places. A wealthy shipbuilder who is an acquaintance from college days approaches Scottie and asks him to follow his wife, Madeleine. He fears she is going insane, maybe even contemplating suicide, because she believes she is possessed by a dead ancestor. Scottie is skeptical, but agrees after he sees the beautiful Madeleine.

After rescuing Madeleine from a leap into San Francisco Bay, he becomes obsessed with her. Later, when because of his vertigo he is unable to save her a second time, he becomes obsessed with re-creating her—and he thinks he's found just the girl for the part, a redhead from Kansas named Judy.

Vertigo is a character-driven story about lost, wandering people—physically restless, spiritually rootless, whose fatal pursuit of an elusive romantic ideal opens them up to exploitation and ultimately emptiness.

The sometime criticism that *Vertigo* is too slow is unfair and unfounded. After the fast chase of the opening, the film begins a slow chase, a long, fluid, vertiginous, dreamlike pursuit of something that doesn't exist, and how could it be otherwise?

From the opening credit sequence to the final image, *Vertigo* is a downward spiral, a long, nightmarish, free fall in one of America's most vertical cities, San Francisco.

Hypnotic and haunting, every aspect of *Vertigo* is affecting—from the script to wardrobe to set design (notice all the reds and greens representing the stop and go of vertigo, the fear of falling and the simultaneous desire to) to Bernhard Herrmann's pitch-perfect soundtrack, and most of all, the performances, particularly that of Jimmy Stewart, who's an underrated dramatic actor with the ability to go to very dark places.

The above excellence is due to the director. All these facets of film were shepherded into being. No one has ever come close to matching Hitchcock's genius in both quality and quantity, and I honestly don't believe anyone ever will.

The auteur theory, which posits that the director is the "author" of a film, applies to Hitch more than any other Hollywood studio filmmaker in history—and he is more the author of *Vertigo* than any other of his pictures.

Like any work of art, it's reductive to say that *Vertigo* is about anything. In a way, it, like all inspired works of art, is about everything (and nothing). But of all its themes, of all that it explores, for me the most devastating is doomed romanticism—the obsessive desire to possess a projected fantasy, the dangerous denial of reality in order to re-create again and again an illusion.

Listen to this haunting exchange:

Judy: Couldn't you like me, just me the way I am? When we first started out, it was so good; we had fun. And... and then you started in on the clothes. Well, I'll wear the darn clothes if you want me to, if, if you'll just, just like me.
Scottie: The color of your hair...
Judy: Oh, no!
Scottie: Judy, please, it can't matter to you.
Judy: If I let you change me, will that do it? If I do what you tell me, will you love me?
Scottie: Yes. Yes.
Judy: All right. All right then, I'll do it. I don't care anymore about me.

Have more sad, tragic, pathetic words ever been penned: "If I let you change me, will that do it? If I do what you tell me, will you love me?"

This exchange calls to mind "the girl" in Hemingway's brilliant "Hills Like White Elephants," who being bullied into an abortion by her American lover, says, "Then I'll do it because I don't care about me anymore."

The notion of self-annihilation in order to be loved is so outlandish, so counterintuitive, yet on display around us every day.

How often have our lovers tried to change us? How often have we let them, hoping, like Judy, that if we do they'll finally love us?

It's not love, of course, which only gives and accepts. In fact, it's the antithesis of love—selfish, conditional, abusive. As Donald Spotto writes, "Perhaps never have exploitation (disguised as love) and self-annihilation (disguised as self-sacrifice) been so tragically presented in film…it amounts to the very definition of false love—a passion which is narcissistic on the one hand and neurotically self-destructive on the other."

In an example of masterful audience manipulation that equals his use of it in *Psycho*, Hitch has us resent Scottie's friend when she attempts to break the spell by mocking the fantasy, and by getting us to desire Judy's transformation into Madeleine nearly as much as Scottie—tell me it doesn't bother you when, returning from the salon, Judy's hair is the color of Madeleine's, but not the style.

As in *Rear Window*, Jimmy Stewart as Scottie Ferguson is Hitch's stand-in, but instead of being a photographer seeing everything through the removed view of a camera lens, this time he's an obsessed director turning a woman into *the* woman—Hitch's ideal blonde remade over and over again through Ingrid Bergman, Anne Baxter, Grace Kelly, Eva Marie Saint, Janet Leigh, Tippi Hedren, and this time, Kim Novak. It's a haunting example of art imitating life imitating art.

Vertigo is a film of authenticity and grandeur, a flawless masterpiece where every single element—every single one—works together perfectly to cast a spell we remain under long after the final shot of Scottie standing on the bell tower, arms spread out, drained, devastated, death-haunted.

People often speak of being disillusioned as a bad thing, but nothing could be further from the truth. Illusions are destructive. Losing them, though often painful, is healthy, loving, freeing. *Vertigo* shows this so purely, so clearly, so unsentimentally, yet compassionately. We can destroy our illusions or be destroyed by them.

I end this piece with the final words of this devastating film: "God have mercy." For it is my deep conviction that whether we rid ourselves of our narcissistic obsessions and precious illusions or cling to them in vertiginous self-destruction, she absolutely will.

The Dark Arts

As a student of Alfred Hitchcock, I've gone back and forth over the years about exactly which film is his best. Each picture is such an amazing artistic achievement—particularly those in the twenty year period from '42-'62—beginning with *Shadow of a Doubt* and ending with *The Birds*—that anointing one the best is extremely challenging. But invariably, *Vertigo*, a truly flawless film, always wins out.

Until now.

Lately, I'm tempted to move *Psycho* from a very secure second into at least a tied-for-first-place position.

The reasons for this are many and varied, but chief among them is Douglas Gordon's *24 Hour Psycho*, an art exhibit consisting entirely of Hitchcock's *Psycho* slowed down to approximately two frames a second, rather than the usual twenty-four, which causes the film to last for exactly twenty-four hours.

By slowing down the film to run at two frames per second, the perfection of every single frame is made more manifest, dramatically demonstrating how the master of suspense was even more a master of mise-en-scene.

Shot with a television crew for $800,000 in black and white on a closed set from November 1959 until February 1960, *Psycho* is one of the greatest cinematic achievements ever—a dark, artistic exploration of the past's influence on the present, the dead's influence on the living, the little traps each of us willingly steps into, identity, gender roles, sexuality, voyeurism, guilt, crime, neurosis, psychosis, and ultimately cinema itself.

Everything in the film means something, is intentional, is thoughtfully and carefully placed in the frame. This is no more true than of the multiple mirrors that not only reveal the disturbing doubling of the split, fractured characters, but require of us, as voyeuristic viewers, serious reflection. But, of course, that's not true, is it? Like the characters in the film, we too can see our image reflected back at us without truly perceiving, we can stare into the abyss without ever realizing all the ways it's staring back. We can "see" this devastating work of art as mere entertainment, this peerless, dark-art masterpiece as a horror film, the progenitor of the modern slasher film.

The splintered narrative of *Psycho* causes us to identify with and change our sympathies for different characters at different times within the film. We *are* Marion Crane, wanting her to have what she wants, wanting her to get away with her crime, to find a way to get out of the trap of her own making, wishing for her a happily ever after. We are her until we can no longer be. Then we become Norman Bates, the poor, lonely man-child with the sick mother in a trap of his own. Hitchcock masterfully manipulates us in ways we think we're morally impervious to. But nowhere is this more thoroughly and profoundly true than when Marion is in her room getting ready for her shower.

Hitchcock shows Norman in the adjoining room remove a painting based on the biblical story of Susannah and the elders—also a story of voyeurism, lust, and blackmail—and peeping at Marion through a hole in the wall as she undresses and prepares to get in the shower. We find his actions sick and demented and condemn him for them. Hitchcock has the camera on a side close-up shot that shows Norman's profile and the light streaming from the hole in the wall into his eye. We condemn him for being so depraved. Then Hitch moves the camera from the side view of Norman to shoot directly into the peephole. Norman's view becomes our view. Suddenly, we see what Norman has been seeing—and we want to, and did while he was looking—and we don't look away. We do the very thing we've been condemning him for—we ourselves split, doubled, splintered in the way Norman and Marion and every character in the film are.

Over and over Hitchcock shows us just how off all our "seeing" is—how erroneous, incomplete, limited, and ultimately wrong our vision and perception are. The film is full of dead eyes—from those of stuffed birds, to murder victims, to the knife-slashed eye of a private eye, to the blank, dead stare of a psychopath. Do we see the world or ourselves any better than Marion or Norman or Mrs. Bates?

No filmmaker in history has ever combined art and entertainment, critical and popular success, light and dark, life and death with the scope and vision of Alfred Hitchcock. With *Psycho* he shows he's a true master of the dark arts—something that becomes more evident when we slow the film, or our contemplation of it, down. There's truth in every frame, if we only have the eyes to see it.

The Truth Is Uglier than You Think

"Treat a hot girl like dirt and she'll stick to you like mud."

This bit of misogynistic venom spit out by Sam from *Slackers* seems less an explanation for his doin' dirt to girls than the philosophy of a generation.

Recent romantic comedies—even those that purport to reveal how guys really think—too often justify, even romanticize sexism and misogyny.

It's alarming how prevalent—check that—how *celebrated* bad behavior is (and not just in rap songs and man-child movies). It's even more alarming how many women allow, even expect it.

Listen to how the studio is promoting the romantic comedy *The Ugly Truth*:

> The battle of the sexes heats up in Columbia Pictures comedy *The Ugly Truth*. Abby Richter (Katherine Heigl) is a romantically challenged morning show producer whose search for Mr. Perfect has left her hopelessly single. She's in for a rude awakening when her bosses team her with Mike Chadway (Gerard Butler), a hardcore TV personality who promises to spill the ugly truth on what makes men and women tick.

The female character is "romantically challenged" and "hopelessly single," the male character is "hardcore" and "truth-telling." Relationships are framed as a battle—or at best a game. The problem with this paradigm is someone has to win and someone has to lose, someone has to dominate and someone has to submit. With the poster picturing the two would-be lovers as the kind of blocky black figures you find on restroom doors with red hearts, the woman's on her head, the man's on his crotch, the battle is framed in the ancient way of men only wanting sex and women having to withhold it until the man surrenders to her terms of marriage—or at least until it's certain he wants more than just her body. In this oppressive and flat out wrong paradigm, men give "love" to get sex and women give sex to get "love"—men are only hounds and women are only virgins or sluts.

Chadway's ugly truth is that men only want sex—lots and lots of sex. And while I only speak for one man, the problem with the caricatured formulation is that it's only partially true. Truth is usually far more nuanced, subtle, complex. Many men, maybe most (even us good guy feminist types) want as much sex as we can get, but that's not the only thing we want. And yet, that is the only thing *some* guys want from *some* girls, and the only thing other guys want from all girls.

The real ugly truth is that our culture is so sexist, Sam's and Mike Chadway's mentalities (and that of the girls they're involved with) shouldn't surprise us. And it's not just them. We have systemic sexism— justified by the powerful, sanctified by the religious, tolerated by all who thoughtlessly accept culture as not only the way things are, but the way things are supposed to be.

The uglier truth is the reason misogynists like Mike Chadway and Sam get so much play is far more a failure of parenting than culture. Succumbing to culture, their parents failed them, as did the parents of all the girls allowing them to treat them badly. By what they said or didn't say, by what they did or didn't do, by what they modeled or by their absence, parents are raising entitled boys to use and abuse, to manipulate and take, and move on; and girls who keep kissing frogs and believing fairytales because they aren't given the tools to imagine anything else.

Obviously, I found *The Ugly Truth* thought-provoking—but more because of its assumptions than what was on the screen. And though it provided a few laughs and a couple of "moments," it's dangerous propaganda.

"Yo, Lister, lighten up. It's a comedy," I can hear some readers saying.

And they'd have a point, but sexism, like racism or classism or homophobia or xenophobia, is only funny when being laughed at, not with.

Here are a few of my truths:

—He's not strong and silent, he's barbaric and emotionally stunted.

—Drama and sick dynamics don't equal desire or passion, just dysfunction.

—It's not just that he's not that into you, he's not into anyone but himself.

—There are far, far, far worse things than being single.

—If a person's not growing and evolving on his or her own, he or she is not going to do it for you (for very long).

—Character is reality, charm is an illusion.

—If you find self-centeredness sexy, you need counseling.

—There's a reason it takes several drinks to do what you're about to do.

—It's not that women don't like sex as much as men, it's that far too many sexual encounters are mostly (if not exclusively) about male satisfaction. (Just because those three minutes were heaven for you doesn't mean it did anything for her.)

—If being treated badly feels good and being treated good feels bad, your operating system has a virus and needs deprogramming and reprogramming.

Like *He's Just Not that Into You, The Ugly Truth* claims to be telling truths about men, about how we are really sex-obsessed users (I, for one am no user), but then ends by reaffirming the sexists' suppositions they claim to be exposing. Both films undermine everything they were saying with unearned, incredible, happy Hollywood endings. The guy who's just not that into you, who keeps giving you all the signs that he only wants sex and not a relationship, realizes by the end of the movie that you're his soul mate, and Mike Chadway is only misogynistic because he has a woman-wounded heart. See, men really do have hearts hidden somewhere behind their enormous erections—all you have to do is persist, keep kissing frogs, keep hoping for the best, keep ignoring the signs, and the guy who says he doesn't want to marry you eventually will, the guy who says he doesn't want a relationship will realize he really does. All you have to do is keep playing his game—or the next guy's game, or the next, or the next, and eventually you'll win. Am I the only one who thinks these are tragedies, not comedies?

Film School

Movies are magic.

Or can be.

The good ones, like all good art, don't merely entertain. They enlighten. They inspire. They educate—an education of heart far more than head.

They transform us.

They challenge us.

They change us.

Of course, there are plenty of people who find film frivolous. Pragmatists, who, unlike me, fail to find meaning in fiction, in made-up stories, in myth and metaphor. It's sad. Stories are sacred. Or can be. They speak to our souls. They have the ability to convey and communicate more truth, more wisdom, more of what matters most, than any other form of communication.

The Film Club, a memoir about movies and other things that really matter, by novelist David Gilmour, demonstrates these truths quietly, but effectively; subtly, but with plenty of profundity.

Gilmour, an unemployed movie critic trying to convince his fifteen-year-old son Jesse to do his homework, realizes Jesse is beginning to view learning as a loathsome chore, and offers him an unconventional deal: Jesse could drop out of school, not work, not pay rent—but he must watch three movies a week of his father's choosing.

Week by week, side by side, father and son watched everything from *True Romance* to *Rosemary's Baby* to *Showgirls*, films by Akira Kurosawa, Martin Scorsese, Brian Depalma, Billy Wilder, and others. The movies got them talking about Jesse's life and his own romantic dramas, with mercurial girlfriends, heart-wrenching breakups, and the kind of obsessive yearning usually seen only in movies.

Through their film club, father and son discussed girls, music, work, drugs, money, love, and friendship—and their own lives changed in surprising ways.

Can watching movies with a novelist/film critic dad really be better than going to school? Is this ingenious parenting or grounds for being declared unfit? You can decide for yourself. My answer? Well, I happen to have a fifteen-year-old son, who truly excels in school—far and away better than I ever did—and, I happen to be a novelist and (something like) a film critic, and I truly believe I could provide him a better education than he could receive virtually anywhere. I'll only add two caveats: 1) Unlike Gilmour, literature would be a big part of my curriculum, and 2) I'd hire a math and science tutor.

Gilmour gambled. He risked a lot in an attempt not just to educate, but to save his son. As he puts it, "The films simply served as an occasion to spend time together, hundreds of hours, as well as a door-opener for all manner of conversational topics—Rebecca (Jesse's girlfriend), Zoloft, dental floss, Vietnam, impotence, cigarettes."

The book is filled with insight and wisdom like:

> The second time you see something is really the *first* time. You need to know how it ends before you can appreciate how beautifully it's put together from the beginning . . .
> It is an example of what films can do, how they can slip past your defenses and really break your heart . . .
> The beautiful girl in the Thunder Bird in *American Graffiti* who keeps disappearing is an example of Proustian contemplation that possession and desire are mutually exclusive, that for the girl to be *the* girl, she must always be pulling away . . .
> You can't be with a woman you can't go to the movies with.

All of which leads Jesse, his son, to certain insights of his own: "It's like when you're watching a film you really love. You don't want somebody trying to be interesting. You want them just to love it."

Gilmour offers much to contemplate about the movies he chooses to reach his son with too. Within just a few introductory paragraphs he reveals interesting information about the movies as well as helping his son (and the reader) have a more meaningful experience with it.

He reveals how Stephen King hated Stanley Kubrick's handling of *The Shining*, said Kubrick made movies to hurt people; how Brando improvised the scene in *On the Waterfront* when he takes the girl's glove and puts it on his hand; how Steven Spielberg made his directing debut with a truck-chase thriller called *Duel*, which he still watches periodically to remind himself of "how he did it"; how Spielberg said, "You have to be young to be so unapologetically sure-footed"; how Howard Hawks said that a good film must have at least "three good scenes and no bad ones." And so much more!

Reading *The Film Club* and reflecting on it reminds me of the way in which I used movies to connect with and educate my daughter over the years—particularly when she was entering early adolescence. We watched all sorts of films—including the horror movies that are such a rite of passage for teenagers—but most of all I designed a cinematic curriculum in feminism, attempting to empower her by showing her just how kickass teenage girls like Buffy Summers and Veronica Mars and Rory Gilmore could be.

This past weekend, my now twenty-year-old kickass daughter came home from college with the textbook from her film class, and we connected over and celebrated cinema all over again as I devoured the tome in our kitchen, in the car (as she drove), and at the table of the Chinese restaurant where we went to lunch. The experience was all the dad of an amazing, kickass co-ed could ask for, and it made me so very grateful that we, like the Gilmours, had started our very own version of the film club so many years ago and that it continues to this day (we even watched *The Killer Inside Me* while she was here).

Gilmour picks some truly great films to share with his son, and the book includes the complete list. I recommend reading the book and watching the movies—and if you can share the experience with someone, form a "film club" of your own, all the better.

Story can be sacred.

Movies can be magic.

Sharing the meaningful ones with our children is nothing short of shamanistic.

A Prescription for Society's Sick Soul

Story can be sacred.

Movies can be magic.

Sharing the meaningful ones with our children is nothing short of shamanistic.

I've long considered what I do as a novelist, as a storyteller, as a teacher, to be shamanistic. If story is sacred, then to be a storyteller is a sacred calling. It's how I view what I do, why I take it so seriously.

Shaman is an anthropological term referring to the spiritual leader of indigenous or native peoples. Shamans are healers and priests and counselors and storytellers.

Shamans are intermediaries or messengers between the human world and the spirit world. They treat ailments and illnesses by mending the soul. By alleviating issues affecting the soul, they restore an individual's entire being to balance and wholeness. They also enter supernatural realms or dimensions to obtain solutions to problems afflicting the community. Shamans visit other worlds to bring guidance to misguided souls, to alleviate suffering caused by soul sickness, removing elements that were never intended to be there. As priests or intermediaries, shamans stand between two worlds—one seen, the other not—serving as a bridge between the two.

A priest or priestess is a go-between, a person straddling two worlds, having a foot planted in each. He or she is a messenger, a representative, an emissary. The same is true of storytellers. We plumb the depths of the underworld and bring back messages. We dig deep beneath the surface and excavate the stories buried there.

I became aware that I was a shaman very early in life, and became active in adolescence—studying story, using story, telling stories, writing stories. My pursuit of my calling has led me to study religion, philosophy, psychology, and story itself. Like so many other shamans I know, I'm not a hobbyist, not doing this just for fun. I'm driven to tell stories, obsessed with story itself and continually improving my storytelling techniques.

It's an odd and interesting time to be a shaman. I'm a shaman in a culture and at a time when serious story and careful, sacred storytelling is devalued, where the novel is increasingly marginalized, yet where, ironically, our need for narrative has never been greater. As a people, as a nation, as a culture, we are soul sick and need the mending, balance, and wholeness only sacred, true story can bring.

There's so much noise in our world, so much inanity, so much that assaults our senses, hearts, and minds. So much. Just so so much.

If we're not very careful to filter input, to guard our quiet time, to thoughtfully and mindfully select our shamans and stories, then the vast majority of what we're assaulted with is shallow, silly, empty, and corrosive. Like junk food, much of what's on offer is wasted calories that neither nourish nor satisfy.

Sacred story is transformative. It speaks to the deepest part of us and calls forth our best selves. The journey of narrative mirrors the journey we're on, and reminds us that it's the epic hero's journey as ancient as time and myth, as old as soul, originating when consciousness did.

For our souls' sake we should honor true shamans and the sacred stories they tell. We should open ourselves up to the magic of story and let it work its wondrous work in us, welcoming the expanding and challenging, emptying and refilling.

Don't settle for substitutes. Seek out true shamans and the magic stories they tell today, and begin sharing your own true, sacred stories with others. If we all got in touch with the shaman in our souls, it would change not only us, and our children, but the whole world entire.

In Praise of Doubt

Certainty is easy. Doubt is difficult.

Certainty is simple. Doubt is complex.

Voltaire said, "Doubt is not a pleasant condition, but certainty is absurd."

Certainty—in the form of personal and philosophical absolutism, religious Fundamentalism, and political fanaticism—is the removal of choice, of the fluid, dynamic nature of life, of the responsibility of thinking, weighing, deciding, of the burden of freedom.

Doubt—in the form of humble openness, thoughtful individuality, egoless emptiness—embraces the limitations of knowledge and perception and lives mindfully and carefully.

To be uncertain about, to hesitate to believe, to question—is how doubt is defined.

Clearly the extremists of our time, whether in politics or religion or the interpersonal arena, don't doubt, but far more frightening is how many of us fail to question all our assumptions—our beliefs, our culture, our relating dynamics, our perceptions, our everything.

Faith is not the absence of doubt. Thoreau said, "Faith keeps many doubts in her pay. If I could not doubt, I should not believe." Faith, which means trust and true faithfulness, not mere belief, embodies doubt. Doubt is an essential part of faith—the part that prevents fanaticism and totalitarianism.

Doubt is severely lacking from one of the severe characters of John Patrick Shanley's *Doubt*—a nun, who when told she hasn't the slightest proof of anything, says, "But I have my certainty."

It's 1964, St. Nicholas in the Bronx. A charismatic priest, Father Flynn, is trying to upend the school's strict customs, which have long been fiercely guarded by Sister Aloysius Beauvier, the iron-gloved principal who believes in the power of fear and discipline. The winds of political change are sweeping through the community, and indeed, the school has just accepted its first black student, Donald Miller. But when Sister James, a hopeful innocent, shares with Sister Aloysius her guilt-inducing suspicion that Father Flynn is paying too much personal attention to Donald, Sister Aloysius sets off on a personal crusade to unearth the truth and to expunge Flynn from the school. Now, without a shard of proof besides her moral certainty, Sister Aloysius locks into a battle of wills with Father Flynn, which threatens to tear apart the community with irrevocable consequences.

Watching *Doubt* the film made me think *Doubt* the play probably worked better, but the film works—and works well—primarily because of the truly riveting performances. Meryl Streep, whom I adore, completely vanishes in the hard, harsh, hateful woman hiding in a habit. And Philip Seymour Hoffman is every bit her match, while Viola Davis and Amy Adams do amazing things with small parts. Of course, the performances are made possible by the writing and are not too hindered by the directing.

There is much to love about *Doubt*, but nothing more than the way it depicts the choice between love and fear, compassion and cynicism.

Father Flynn's God is one of love. He says, "There are people who go after your humanity. They tell you that the light in your heart is a weakness. Don't believe it. It's an old tactic of cruel people to kill kindness in the name of virtue. There's nothing wrong with love."

Sister Aloysius's God is one of rigid rules and wrath. When asked where her compassion was, she responds, "Nowhere you can get at it." She's tyrannical, intolerant of the new, the different—including Christmas songs, ballpoint pens, and cough drops, which she calls candy by another name. She may or may not be right about Father Flynn, but she's wrong about nearly everything else.

Doubt is a very fine film—a thought-provoking parable that dramatizes love and fear, differing images of God, and the oppression that much of male-dominated religion and culture placed (and continues to place) on women, but where it truly excels is in demonstrating the need for the divine presence of doubt.

Friends and Lovers

They say a friend will help you move and a best friend will help you move a body.

They also say true love is friendship set afire.

Of course, anything on fire has the potential to burn up or, worse, burn out, which is why it seems more and more moderns are no longer risking love. Even many who are in relationships reserve so much of themselves, hold back so much of their hearts, have such enormously tall, thick fortresses around their secret selves that they sabotage a relationship before the very first date.

More and more, at least in word and deed if not heart and mind, they are choosing a new paradigm of interaction without true intimacy—pseudo friends with the benefit of pseudo sex.

Can a friend be a lover? What is the difference between the two? Can former lovers remain friends? Can sex be unemotional, unencumbered by anything other than the physical?

The latest movie to explore these questions, following hard on the heels of *No Strings Attached*, is *Friends with Benefits*—and it does so with much more humor, chemistry, and intelligence than the earlier film.

A young female headhunter (Mila Kunis) in New York convinces a potential recruit (Justin Timberlake) to leave his job in San

Francisco behind and accept a job in the big apple. Despite an attraction
to each other, both realize they're everything they've been running from
in a relationship and decide to become friends…with benefits. It's the
perfect arrangement. Or is it?

This film is elevated by the writing, by the chemistry of its
actors, by not trying to be something it's not, by its humor, and, most of
all, by Mila Kunis, who truly shines.

Though this is a Hollywood romance that criticizes the clichés
of Hollywood romances, I found the fact that it went on to commit
those same clichés mostly forgivable—partially because of the way they
went about it, but mostly because the movie works. And the thing about
true love is it makes clichés of us all. Suddenly, we're moved by sappy,
silly movies. Incredibly, radio love songs reveal our truest feelings like
nothing else can. If we let it, love makes fools of us all—the happiest,
luckiest, best of fools. Of course, the true, tragical fool is the one who
fails to become love's fool.

Friends make the best lovers. And I would never want a lover
who wasn't also a best friend. If you trace the etymology of the word
friend, in nearly every language it leads you back to the word *love*. A friend
is someone we love.

How can you know when you've found the right combination
of friend and lover? According to *Friends with Benefits*, when the person
you want to spend Friday night with is also the person you want to
spend all day Saturday with.

To my way of thinking, lovers should be friends first—and last.

I hope it goes without saying I'm not advocating allowing abuse,
and certainly there's a place for boundaries where addiction or mental
illness exists. I only mean that love is all, and that there is no justification
for closing our hearts to it.

There's no question that Eros makes us all a little mad. Passion,
romance, sex, souls wantonly connecting are potent and powerful
intoxicants—ones we should all deeply and extravagantly enjoy—but we
can only safely drink to drunkenness on desire when our true sobriety
is the stabilizing surety of true charity, of the certainty that we are
unconditionally loved.

Like love, friendship is a commitment, a way of life. Perhaps
former lovers can't be best friends, but they can be friends. I've
never understood how people who once loved each other can now
say they don't. Either they never did really love each other with true,

unconditional love, or they've let pain and disappointment turn to bitterness and unforgiveness and choke out love. Love—real, pure love—is not something we fall into our out of.

Love is messy. Love is costly. Love, like life, is suffering. But there's no better way to live.

Don't detach. Engage.

If true love is friendship set afire, we're going to get burned. This is not theoretical, not fanciful. I know what I'm talking about. My heart is charred right now. And I wouldn't have it any other way.

Don't lock your heart in a fireproof box. Smolder. Burn. Love both friends and lovers with abandon. Let the flame of love engulf you to consumption. I challenge you to find a better way to live this too-short life.

Alone with All That Can Happen

The morning after watching *Solitary Man*, I woke up feeling utterly and completely alone. I'm pretty sure it had nothing to do with the movie—I often experience an intense sense of isolation—but the timing was interesting and thought-provoking.

Being alone isn't the same as being lonely. Many times I feel the most connected when I am most alone—something Lord Byron captured so beautifully in his phrase, "In solitude, where we are least alone."

Being with others isn't the same as not being lonely. Certain people, certain settings and situations, make me feel more lonely, not less. A social gathering involving small talk, cocktail chatter, mundane, surfaces inanities—and what social gathering doesn't include such things—usually makes me feel far more isolated and alone than when I'm actually by myself.

Whether we're alone or with others, in one sense we're always ultimately alone. As Thomas Wolfe said, "Loneliness is and always has been the central and inevitable experience of every human."

Even as we appear to be sharing the same experiences—including intensely intimate experiences like making love or sharing a meal or talking about God—we're always having our own unique experience. Oscar Wilde's observation that there are as many publics as there are people is true of everything. It's why I say there are some six and half billion gods. No two of us have identical notions of what the word *god* means. So whatever God is and is not, we're left with our beliefs and perceptions, and though heavily influenced by culture and family, indoctrination and education, they're still utterly and uniquely only our own.

Beneath all our labels, beyond all our associations and group identities, it's just us. Ultimately alone. Solitary us. Yet there is an us. We are part of a planet, a species, an interdependent system. We are able to connect, to touch each others' souls, be inside one another in profound and meaningful ways. At this very moment, you and I are having a personal, intimate, (hopefully) meaningful exchange. I am offering you the water of my words and you are drinking them in.

And yet. And yet.

Even as we have truly deep and intensely intimate connections, we remain, in a very real and certain sense, alone. And it's out of that aloneness, that sometimes painful experience of isolation, we reach out—out of our solitude—to an other.

Solitary means "being, living, or going alone or without companions; saddened by isolation; keeping a prisoner apart from others; being at once single and isolated; occurring singly and not as part of a group or cluster."

Occurring singly and not being part of a group is a good thing. Emerson said, "Whoso would be a man must be a nonconformist."

In one sense, the more evolved and self-actualized, the more true to our quiddity, the more we refuse to conform, the more alone we will be—less able to fit, less a part of group think and group speak. We will not benefit from the safety found in numbers. But this evolution of our beings will also simultaneously, counterintuitively, lead us to a greater awareness of our connectedness with all people, with all things. Connected at very deep levels; completely unconnected at shallower levels.

These are thoughts I'm having as I think of solitude and my experience in proximity to the film. They are not necessarily in the film except in very implicit ways. Ben Kalmen's solitude originates from the deepest, most profound place—his mortality—but his outward isolation isn't from self-actualization, but its opposite, not out of love, but fear.

Solitary Man tells the story of Ben Kalmen, a fifty-something New Yorker and former successful car dealer, who through his own bad choices lost his entire business.

When the film opens, Ben's on the verge of a comeback, but some of the same motivations that led to his demise are threatening to take him down again. He's divorced from Nancy, his college sweetheart and the one person who knows him better than anyone. Although he still finds the time to hang out with his daughter, Susan, and his adoring grandson, she breaks off contact when she discovers he's seeing one of her friends. His girlfriend, Jordan, is the daughter of a very influential businessman who's on the board of a major auto manufacturer.

If Ben can just keep his hubris in check for a little while longer, he will be back as big as ever. But circumstances place him in very close proximity with the one girl he shouldn't touch, throwing everything into jeopardy.

Solitary Man is solid story elevated by great performances. Michael Douglas is brilliant as Ben, and the other players hovering around the edges of his solitariness hang right there with him.

Ben's isolation is more an acting out, a childish, defensive way of actually isolating others that leads him to be isolated himself. He's a solitary man because of bad behavior, because he's incapable of intimacy.

The sense of isolation—even the experience itself—is part of the human condition. It is not the same as never connecting, as being unable or unwilling to—which seems the case for Ben.

Even in our ultimate aloneness we can connect with others. In fact, we can connect because of it, through it. Sharing our feelings of isolation with another human who is open about his or her own feelings of separation frees us from our solitary confinement prison cell.

Solitude is a good and necessary part of existence. We are our best selves when we have the time and space to be ourselves, to just be—in the beauty and stillness of silence and solitude. Einstein said, "I lived in solitude in the country and noticed how the monotony of a quiet life stimulates the creative mind."

It comes down to balance. Too much or too little or the wrong kind of solitude negatively impacts our souls. Finding trusted friends who are themselves seeking this same balance and committing to each other to aid in the process is invaluable. As Rilke so wisely put it, "I hold this to be the highest task for a bond between two people: that each protects the solitude of the other."

Learn from Ben's mistakes. Identify those in your life who

protect your good solitude and make sure you're protecting theirs. And in those times when you feel all alone, be fully present, and don't just be alone. Be alone with the promise and possibility of all that can happen.

My Long, Happy Love Affair

I fell in love in Tulsa, Oklahoma in 1994.

It started out as a one-night stand, but blossomed into a passionate love affair that has been happily going on for fifteen years now.

In honor of National Coming Out Day (and with love and support for all my GLBT brothers and sisters), I'm going to use this column to confess my love for a man.

I first fell in love with Richard Curtis while experiencing his delightful film *Four Weddings and a Funeral*.

I was alone in Tulsa with a free evening, and had been hearing good things about this indie British film sweeping the states. The theater was packed, and though I've never liked group dates, the presence of the crowd was powerless to prevent me from finding a soul mate.

Though his films are often laugh-out-loud hilarious, he has a smart, witty way of capturing moments that are both realistic and wildly romantic. His characters are multi-faceted and complex, and easy to identify with, but mostly they are charming. He writes about good, guileless everymen and women trying to connect, trying to matter, wanting to be everything to someone. As one of his characters offers in his toast, "True love. In whatever shape or form it may come. May we all in our dotage be proud to say, 'I was adored once too.'"

Four Weddings and a Funeral follows the fortunes of Charles (Hugh Grant) and his friends as they wonder if they will ever find true love. Charles thinks he's found his best chance with Carrie, an American he meets at the wedding of a mutual friend, but, as Shakespeare said, "the course of true love never did run straight."

Romantic comedies, like most genre works, often fail to get the critical recognition they deserve (though *Four Weddings and a Funeral* did receive an Oscar nomination for best picture), and are instead dismissed out of hand for being unrealistic. And, of course, there's no dearth of crass, clichéd examples of so-called genre works, but like James Lee Burke or P.D. James in the crime fiction field or Cormac McCarthy in the Western field, Curtis represents the very best of the genre—he's so good, in fact, he transcends genre categorizations.

Speaking about this unfortunate reality, Curtis said, "If you write a story about a soldier going AWOL and kidnapping a pregnant woman and finally shooting her in the head, it's called searingly realistic, even though it's never happened in the history of mankind. Whereas if you write about two people falling in love, which happens about a million times a day all over the world, for some reason or another, you're accused of writing something unrealistic and sentimental."

Weddings and funerals are seminal moments in life—a time to live and a time to die, a time to rejoice and a time to mourn, and Curtis uses them masterfully for both laughs and tears.

Perhaps the most piercing moment of the film is at its only funeral when the deceased man's lover quotes a W.H. Auden poem.

Upon leaving the theater, so moved, so in love, so heady with the world-fading-oneness that love (and infatuation) brings, I drove straight to the first bookstore I could find and bought Vintage International's edition of the *Collected Poems of W.H. Auden*, and when I pulled that book off my shelf while writing this, I discovered a bookmark from Novel Idea Bookstore, 7104 S. Sheridan, Tulsa OK, fifteen years later still marking the page with this poem:

> Stop all the clocks, cut off the telephone,
> Prevent the dog from barking with a juicy bone,
> Silence the pianos and with muffled drum
> Bring out the coffin, let the mourners come.

Let aeroplanes circle moaning overhead
Scribbling on the sky the message He is Dead.
Put crepe bows round the white necks of the public
doves,
Let the traffic policemen wear black cotton gloves.

He was my North, my South, my East and West,
My working week and my Sunday rest,
My noon, my midnight, my talk, my song;
I thought that love would last forever: I was wrong.

The stars are not wanted now; put out every one,
Pack up the moon and dismantle the sun,
Pour away the ocean and sweep up the woods;
For nothing now can ever come to any good.

My love affair with Richard Curtis has only intensified over the
years—through *Notting Hill*, *Love Actually*, and *The Girl in the Café*, but it
all began many years ago in Tulsa, Oklahoma, with *Four Weddings and a
Funeral.*
I'd like to invite you to a wedding—a few weddings, in fact (and
a non-wedding and a funeral). If you missed the film or just haven't seen
it in a while, do yourself a favor and find it. I'm about to watch it again
for what must be nearly the fifteenth time, and can think of no better
way to celebrate my *Four Weddings and a Funeral* anniversary.

Coloring Outside the
Lines in Pleasantville

Recently, as someone was criticizing my novels for what they called "inappropriate content," I suddenly felt like I was living in Pleasantville, and shortly afterward went back and watched Gary Ross's profound 1998 film.

Over a decade after I first saw it, *Pleasantville* holds up well, and is just as relevant. If you haven't seen it, or if it's been a while, consider taking a trip across the universe to visit Pleasantville.

Pleasantville is a colorless, lifeless, pointless place where repressed people pretend the world is the way they want it to be.

A brother and sister (twins, David and Jennifer) from the 1990s are transported through their television set into the 1950s-style black-and-white television show *Pleasantville*. Here, they have loving, if robotic, parents, values that seem old fashioned, and an overwhelming amount of innocence, even naiveté. Not sure how to get home, they integrate themselves into this bland society as well as they can and slowly begin a revolution.

The revolution they start, like all revolutions, begins with freedom—freedom of thought, freedom of expression, freedom to be.

Fear imprisons. Love liberates.

We were created to be autonomous, formed to be free (we were created to connect too, but out of freedom). We can't be who we're really meant to be without being free.

Perhaps the single greatest tragedy of life is how frequently, how readily, how willingly we give away our freedom.

We do it out of fear. We trade our most precious birthright for a false sense of security and the safety-in-numbers uniformity the prophets of fear peddle.

Of course, like many of us, the people of Pleasantville don't know they're not free. So mired in the quicksand of culture are they, they are no longer conscious.

In Pleasantville, everyone is asleep, all dreaming the same boring dream.

But David and Jennifer wake them up.

The awakening of Pleasantville is accomplished by a variety of means—all having to do with freedom.

It begins with questions. Jennifer asks what's outside of Pleasantville—something no citizen of Pleasantville had ever even thought of. For them, Pleasantville is the world entire, in the same way we often think that our world, our way of seeing the world, is all there is. We can never be completely free until we question everything—every assumption, every belief, everything every authority ever told us. Questioning is key to enlightenment. Questions are far, far more important than answers.

Then, Jennifer introduces Pleasantvillians to sex. You can't have a revolution without sex. Like questioning, people seem to be particularly fearful of sex—of sex in general, of sexual freedom in particular—especially that of young people and women. The residual Puritanism so prevalent in our culture has people afraid of their sexuality. But the awesome power of sex should be respected, revered, not feared. Sex is, or can be, a revelation, a revolution. Rarely does one have a true spiritual or creative awakening that does not include, or was not inspired by, a sexual one.

The revolution in Pleasantville continues when David and Jennifer introduce books and reading. Nothing equals freedom like the writing and publishing and reading of books. The sharing of ideas, the intellectual intercourse that occurs between writer and reader in the bedroom of a book, is truly one of the highlights of being human, and this, too, is revolutionary—both personally and politically. No wonder the establishment (those that benefit most from the domination system and the sleeping of the masses) wants to ban and burn books.

Eventually, David introduces art to the pale people of Pleasantville, and the revolution really begins to swell. Vivid colors, unique expressions, the artistic appreciation of the female form, and the powers that be come undone.

Then, there are choices in music and food and fashion.

Suddenly, people are bursting into full color, experiencing their lives fully awake for the first time. How does the establishment respond? By closing the library and lovers' lane, by outlawing all colors but black and white and gray, by having book burnings and destroying any and all acts of art, all expressions of creativity.

Those in power are oppressive—ever trying to cling to the power they have and acquire more. But the real problem in Pleasantville—as in Pottersville as in Niceville as in ourville—isn't oppression so much as repression.

Of all the crimes against humanity, repression is one of the most insidious. Unlike oppression, which can be an exclusively external force, repression involves complicity on the part of the repressed.

True repression—like the systemic and institutional sexism, racism, and homophobia that leads to desperation, frustration, and self-loathing—is not only an external condition but must be so internalized that those imprisoned in it become co-conspirators—jailers in their own captivity.

If there's anything missing from the awakenings in Gary Ross's *Pleasantville*, it's religious awakening. Though everything that happened constitutes a spiritual awakening, I wish Ross would have depicted a religious awakening too—the reformations and counter-reformations that make up the best of religious traditions. Fundamentalists and literalists of every tradition claim theirs is the only way to be right or orthodox, but the very religion they pervert wouldn't exist had someone not questioned and challenged and reformed the one that came before it.

In the great irony of human history, God created us to be free, insists on our absolute freedom (has God ever made you do anything?), yet it is out of fear of God that so many surrender their freedom. False religion teaches followers to be afraid—afraid to be human, afraid to mess up, afraid to do anything but conform to its fear-based rules. But God is not to be feared. God is love. Perfect love, in fact—the very antithesis of fear.

The good news is we are loved and accepted unconditionally. We have nothing to fear. Be free. Be yourself. Relax. Rest. Stop resisting. Love's not going anywhere. Be creative. It's okay to use all the crayons in your box, okay to color outside the lines.

Like the people of Pleasantville, intellectual, sexual, religious, artistic repression is killing us. It's a slow suicide of the soul, a drifting off into a sleepy stupor that only waking up and being free can cure.

Awakening.

You and I hold the key to our own prison cells.

Like the Buddha beneath the bodhi tree, Moses in the wilderness, Jesus in the desert, we must awaken. With openness and freedom, we must explore, experiment, experience, be—knowing that as we do, life isn't always pleasant and was never intended to be. Awakening, being free, is a sometimes chaotic, wild, messy process, requiring that we take risks, explore, experiment, color outside the lines, and fail, but there's no other way to be fully human, no other way to achieve enlightenment.

The New Obstacles of Modern Romance

All you need to make a romance is a guy, a girl, and some obstacles.

Obviously, there's a bit more to it than that, particularly if it is to be done well, but I'm playing off of Jean-Luc Godard's famous comment that "all you need to make a movie is a girl and a gun."

I began thinking about true love's obstacles after watching *Bright Star* and *Romeo and Juliet* on the same day.

Bright Star is Jane Campion's 2009 film based on the last three years of the life of poet John Keats and his romantic relationship with Fanny Brawne.

The version of *Romeo and Juliet* I watched, my favorite Shakespeare adaptation and one of my all-time favorite films, is Franco Zeffirelli's 1968 masterpiece staring Leonard Whiting and Olivia Hussey.

The many obstacles to love faced by the most famous teenage lovers in history are well known—their star-crossed connection doomed from the jump because their only love sprang from their only hate, their secret marriage, Romeo's killing of Juliet's cousin, Juliet's forced marriage to another man, and so on and so on until they are both dead. As obstacles go, these aren't at all bad. Not at all.

Of course, those of John Keats and Fanny Brawne are pretty impressive too. The two are of different classes in a time when that kind of thing really mattered. He couldn't afford to marry, couldn't support himself, let alone a wife. And finally, he catches his death of cold and is sick for a lengthy period and then, well, watch the movie.

I found *Bright Star* moving and passionate, smart and romantic. Jane Campion is a fantastic director and, as usual, she has made a stunningly beautiful film.

This was the first time I've seen *Romeo and Juliet* in HD and it was exquisite. The forty-three-year-old film holds up extremely well. As far as I'm concerned, there will never be a better Juliet than teenaged Olivia Hussey. I first saw the film when I was maybe eight or ten and was so moved by it that I was sick for days afterwards.

Both *Romeo and Juliet* and *Bright Star* are intensely romantic and tragic, and as in the case of our own epic adventures, death has the final word. And though I believe as the Song of Songs says that "love is as strong as death," as far as we know and as far as we can see, it is the insurmountable obstacle of this life and, therefore, its loves.

Classic love stories have classic obstacles—cultural taboos, such as class, caste, money, power, race, religion, gender roles, sexual orientation, etc.—powerful enough to keep all but the strongest soul mates from their fates.

But what do we have today? What possible credible obstacles do modern members of educated, liberal democracies have? For many of us, the dragons of class, race, religious, sexual, and financial impediments have been slain. What's left?

What are the new obstacles?

As enjoyable and inspiring and moving as I found the two films, I found myself thinking more about the new modern obstacles and concluded that in the absence of outward, societal obstacles and taboos, we have created our own largely internal ones for the narratives inside our heads and the postmodern stories we tell and live.

The new Capulets and Montagues and cultural taboos are neuroses and narcissism, ambivalence and the tyranny of too many choices. External demons have become inner ones. We don't have impediments as much as issues. Abandonment issues. Daddy issues. Mommy issues. Commitment issues. And on and on issue ad infinitum.

And I don't think it's a coincidence we have these now that we don't have the others.

Newfound freedom causes a vacuum that the insecure rush to fill.

Most modern romances, with the exception of Richard Curtis's brilliant *Notting Hill*, which was about the new and very modern obstacle of celebrity, are more about ambivalence than much of anything else, about self-involved characters who are afraid, who really don't want relationships. Sure, they want sex, they want interaction, but not intimacy, not strings, not entanglement, not love, not commitment. And I think this is a case of art imitating life, of our modern stories reflecting our modern condition, of avoidance and ambiguity, of fear and ambivalence, of a new level of self-centeredness, of external obstacles being replaced by internal issues, whether real, imagined, or invented, that net the same result—the tragic thwarting of love. But it seems far more significant and substantial when the obstacle is that of an entire repressed culture than a character merely being unable to make up her mind.

It's Complicated

Last week my dear friend, John Bridges, was planning to see *It's Complicated* when he read my review of *Up in the Air* and decided to see it instead. When he told me what he planned to do, I said that I suspected *It's Complicated* would be more entertaining, but that *Up in the Air* was probably the better, more substantive film. I'm humbled and honored that he trusts my recommendations, and I couldn't help but think of him as I watched *It's Complicated* a few days later, pleasantly surprised at how good it was. It's funny and charming and highly entertaining—but not just. It also manages to deliver some insight and provoke some thought.

So, John, now I'm recommending you see *It's Complicated*, and for all of us, I recommend we set our Facebook relationship statuses to "It's Complicated." After all, when have relationships ever not been?

Jane Adler (Meryl Streep) is the mother of three grown kids, owns a thriving Santa Barbara bakery/restaurant and has—after a decade of divorce—an amicable relationship with her ex-husband, attorney Jake (Alec Baldwin). But when Jane and Jake find themselves out of town for their son's college graduation, things start to get complicated. An innocent meal together leads to several bottles of wine, which in turn becomes a laugh-filled evening of memories about their nineteen-year marriage…and then to an impulsive affair. With Jake remarried to the much younger Agness (Lake Bell), Jane is now, of all things, the other woman. Caught in the middle of this renewed romance is Adam (Steve Martin), an architect hired to remodel Jane's kitchen. Also divorced, Adam starts to fall for Jane, but soon realizes he's become part of an unusual love triangle. Should Jane and Jake move on with their separate lives, or has the passage of time made them realize that they really are better together than apart? It's…complicated.

Nancy Myers, an extremely talented writer/director, who two years ago wrote and directed one of my all-time favorite Christmas movies, *The Holiday*, proves once again that Hollywood needs far more women in front of and behind the camera. Her writing is clever, witty, and by turns, poignant and hysterical, and whether paired with Meryl Streep, Diane Keaton, Cameron Diaz, or Kate Winslet, she gives moviegoers mature, powerful, multi-faceted women not seen nearly often enough at the Cineplex (art house and indie theaters are a different matter, but good luck finding one). And that's the thing. Myers is bringing feminism to the masses—a certain type of feminism, mostly light-hearted, comedic, meant-to-entertain-first, but a real feminism to be sure. And she's mastered (or should I say mistressed) the romantic comedy, which she understands in the context of contemporary culture. "There's a hardening of the culture," she said. "Reality TV has lowered the standards of entertainment. You're left wondering about the legitimacy of relationships. It's probably harder to entertain the same people with a more classic form of writing, and romantic comedies are a classic genre."

Film and literature are rife with tales of adultery—from King David and Bathsheba, whose relationship ultimately led to *Jesus of Nazareth*, to *The Scarlet Letter*, to *Anna Karenina*, to *Brief Encounter*, to *The End of the Affair*—but in both film and literature, most tales of not-entirely unattached lovers are dramas, if not melodramas, involving guilt-ridden, tortured, ultimately doomed souls, who are punished for what is seen as religious and cultural and personal transgression. But Myers shows that affairs—which are often, among other things, fun—can be funny, life-affirming, and highly entertaining experiences. She does this, in part, by making the lovers formerly married, which gives them a culturally sanctioned relationship in the past and a prior claim over their current lovers. And isn't that how most people feel: "He was mine first." "She belonged to me before you even knew her!"

Justification and palatability aside, the movie is about adultery.

John Updike saw adultery—whether in life or only art, I do not know, though I suspect both—as "an imaginative quest," and, as one of his characters put it, "a way of giving yourself adventures, of getting out in the world and seeking knowledge." The psychoanalyst Wilhelm Reich actually claims "the only social purpose of compulsory marriage for life is to produce submissive personality types that mass society requires," and that "repressing sexual curiosity leads to general intellectual atrophy, including loss of power to rebel," which has led Laura Kipnis, author of *Against Love* and *The Female Thing* to assert that "adultery is actually an act of cultural rebellion" and that "monogamy turns nice people into petty dictators and household tyrants." Radical notions? Perhaps, but we're all swimming around in the water of culture like fish who don't know what water is, and our best hope of awareness, enlightenment, and compassion is to entertain all questions. And no one should question culture and marriage and roles and identity more than women. Thankful many are—from Myers to Kipnis to Anne Kingston, author of *The Meaning of Wife*. And, as Thomas Moore, author of *Care of the Soul* teaches, none of this need be taken literally.

I really appreciate what Myers has done here. True, *It's Complicated* could have been far more complicated, but for a mainstream romantic comedy, it at least has audience sympathies in the right places. The film could've dealt with affairs in a more nuanced, less adulterous way—take out lying and cheating, and things are less complicated and far more honorable—but it's a comedy and a big commercial-studio film, and given that, it's very, very good.

Forget "greatest living actress." It's time to refer to Meryl Streep as what she is—the greatest actress in history. And at sixty-something, could she be any more beautiful, attractive, strong, sexy?

Alec Baldwin and Steve Martin turn in fine, admirable performances, both bringing their characters to life with certain appeals for Meryl Streep's Jane Adler, but clearly she is out of their league. I won't tell you which man Jane chooses, only that to make things truly complicated, she should've kept both men as friends and lovers. Jane could certainly handle it. And Meryl, well, Meryl could handle an entire harem—or (since there's not a word for a female harem, which is telling, is it not?) a stable.

Life and love and relationships are complicated enough to make one want to cry, but perhaps a better approach is laughter. Myers certainly makes a convincing argument.

Perchance to Dream

To sleep, perchance to dream—ay, there's the rub:
For in that sleep of death what dreams may come.

For all we know—or think we do—we know very little about
dreams. Of course, the truth is, we know very little about much of
anything, but some things are harder to fake than others.

Dreams can be defined as a succession of images, sounds, or
emotions the mind experiences during sleep, but that doesn't even begin
it.

Dreams are mystical and spiritual, ineffable and inexplicable,
which is why I take issue with Freud's claim in *The Interpretation of Dreams*
that he can "demonstrate that there is a psychological technique which
makes it possible to interpret dreams, and that on the application of this
technique, every dream will reveal itself as a psychological structure, full
of significance, and one which may be assigned to a specific place in the
psychic activities of the waking state."

Dreams are mysteries. Any interpretation is at best only partially
correct.

Dreams can be instructive and inspiring, but in the way all
mysterious things (God, the universe, art, life, death) are—in subtle,
lyrical, non-literal, largely metaphorical ways.

Dreams are also rich material for story. Fiction, whether on page or screen, is like a dream. My experience with writing fiction—particularly the novel—is that it is very much like entering a kind of dream state, and I, to varying degrees, remain in it until the novel is born.

It occurred to me that dreams play significant roles in three out of four of my most recent novels.

Dreams are the subject and the setting for acclaimed filmmaker Christopher Nolan's new movie, *Inception*—an original sci-fi actioner that travels around the globe and into the intimate and infinite world of dreams. Dom Cobb (Leonardo DiCaprio) is a skilled thief, the absolute best in the dangerous art of extraction, stealing valuable secrets from deep within the subconscious during the dream state, when the mind is at its most vulnerable. Cobb's rare ability has made him a coveted player in this treacherous new world of corporate espionage, but it has also made him an international fugitive and cost him everything he has ever loved.

Now Cobb is being offered a chance at redemption. One last job could give him his life back, but only if he can accomplish the impossible—inception. Instead of the perfect heist, Cobb and his team of specialists have to pull off the reverse: their task is not to steal an idea but to plant one. If they succeed, it could be the perfect crime. But no amount of careful planning or expertise can prepare the team for the dangerous enemy that seems to predict their every move—an enemy that only Cobb could have seen coming.

Though one of the most well-made and entertaining films of this disappointing summer at the Cineplex, *Inception* was not as good as I wanted it to be.

Sure, it demonstrates a brilliant filmmaker at work. It's as well constructed a movie as you're likely to see. It's interesting and exciting and intense, but it has no soul.

It's visually stunning, intellectually engaging, but emotionally unfulfilling. A puzzle, a logicians labyrinth. Clever. Cold. Cerebral. I wanted to care for the characters—enjoy the movie on more than an intellectual level—but there was no heart, no warmth, no spirit.

And I wish *Inception* had been more dreamlike, more random and hazy and nonlinear. For all its talk about and delving into dreams, there's very little in it that feels like anyone is actually dreaming. I felt it could really have used the hypnotic touch of a director like David Lynch.

Mulholland Drive has far more of the dewy residue of dream state than does *Inception*.

Both times I watched *Inception*, I thought of another dream-like movie, *What Dreams May Come*—and though it's more about the dreams that come when we've shuffled off this mortal coil, it makes a quite convincing case that those dreams are more like the ones we have in our beds at night or in our heads during the day than we realize.

Though I've seen *What Dreams May Come* several times, I decided to watch it again while writing this, and I discovered that it's even better than I remembered. A lot better.

I had also forgotten how beautiful and extraordinary Annabella Sciorra is and what a tour de force her amazing performance is in this film. Watching her served to heighten how weak the poorly cast Ellen Page is in *Inception*.

Watch any scene in *What Dreams May Come* and you'll find more true, convincing human emotion than in all of *Inception*.

What Dreams May Come is a gorgeous film, a work of art, filled with and about art. It's magical and mystical and beautiful. In short, it's a dream. It's a stunning work of imagination about life and death, but most of all it's about love and loss. It's profound and says some interesting things about the world to come—something like "as below, so above," we create our lives in the afterlife in the same way we do in this present life, that if something is true in our minds, it is true. As the person who wrote the phrase "what dreams may come" says, "Nothing is either good or bad, but thinking makes it so."

What Dreams May Come is about things dreams are made of—twins, soul mates, second chances, not giving up, winning when you lose and losing when you win. It's filled with the things that fill dreams. It's inspiring and inspiriting—and everything that *Inception* is not.

It's not that *Inception* is bad. It's not. It's quite good, and as for well-crafted, thoughtful, and thought-provoking entertainment in theaters right now, it nears the top of the list of limited choices. In fact, I recommend it.

I recommend both movies, but for very different reasons. If you want to see a high-quality timepiece at work, go see the Swiss watch-like *Inception*. Its precision and brilliance are beautiful to behold. But if you want to spend time with something truly timeless, watch *What Dreams May Come*, and as you do, open your mind and heart and embrace the dream of life taking place in the mind of God.

Rocket Man

Making connections in modern American culture is increasingly difficult. There's plenty of noise—cocktail chatter, small talk, so much sound and fury that ultimately signifies nothing, but there's very little deep soul-to-soul connecting. In our frenetic activity, we bump into each other, but don't really stop, don't really listen, don't really have meaningful exchanges—we commit social hit-and-runs and call them relationships.

It's not that we don't want to connect. I honestly think we're dying to. Craigslist's personals have an entire category devoted to Missed Connections, and though most of them appear to be written by horny people trying to find someone based purely on how they look, I think it underscores a deep longing for far, far more than just hookin' up.

We are lonely. We are longing.

Has it always been this way? There's no way for me to know, but I suspect that, though earlier times were more communal, caring, connected, true naked-and-safe connection has always been rare. The good old days get idealized and romanticized, but perhaps in this way, in rootedness and belonging, they actually were gooder.

There are many reasons for our separation and isolation, and far smarter people than me have written books about them (including *Bowling Alone* by Robert Putnam and *Loneliness as a Way of Life* by

Thomas Dumm), but as complicated as the condition is (and I truly believe it is extremely complicated), I tend to think the single biggest contributing factor is parenting. We live in a time of absurd over and underparenting—two extremes that might actually produce similar results. Could it be that neglect, insignificant-to-the-universe parenting on one end of the spectrum and overindulgence, center-of-the-universe parenting on the other create kids who become adults who can't connect? The net result of feeling unworthy or too worthy of bonding is the same, is it not? How many times have we attempted to make a real connection with someone only to find out that they're too self-absorbed and narcissistic or too absent a sense of self and wounded for it to be even remotely possible?

Ryan Bingham, the central character of Jason Reitman's timely, insightful new film, *Up in the Air*, finds it nearly impossible to make connections. His job is to fire people from theirs, and he flies all over the country to do it. He has no trouble with connecting flights—he never misses them, but making connections with other human beings is a different story.

In the film, Bingham's life in the air is threatened just before he is about to reach ten million frequent flyer miles and just after he's met his female frequent flyer soul mate. The anguish, hostility, and despair of his "clients" have left him falsely compassionate, living out of a suitcase, and loving his above-it-all position. When his boss hires arrogant young Natalie, she develops a method of video conferencing that will allow termination without ever leaving the office—threatening Bingham's very existence. Determined to show the naive girl the error of her logic, Ryan takes her on one of his cross-country firing expeditions, but as she starts to realize the disheartening realities of her profession, he gets a glimpse of the emptiness of his way of life.

Ray Bingham is a rocket man. Elton John's song could've been written for him.

> It's lonely out in space
> On such a timeless flight
> And I think it's gonna be a long long time
> Till touchdown brings me round again to find
> I'm not the man they think I am at home
> Oh no no no I'm a rocket man
> Rocket man burning out his fuse up here alone

Here's Rocket Man Ray's philosophy :

How much does your life weigh? Imagine for a second that you're carrying a backpack. I want you to pack it with all the stuff that you have in your life…you start with the little things. The shelves, the drawers, the knickknacks, then you start adding larger stuff. Clothes, tabletop appliances, lamps, your TV…the backpack should be getting pretty heavy now. You go bigger. Your couch, your car, your home…I want you to stuff it all into that backpack. Now I want you to fill it with people. Start with casual acquaintances, friends of friends, folks around the office…and then you move into the people you trust with your most intimate secrets. Your brothers, your sisters, your children, your parents and finally your husband, your wife, your boyfriend, your girlfriend. You get them into that backpack, feel the weight of that bag. Make no mistake your relationships are the heaviest components in your life. All those negotiations and arguments and secrets, the compromises. The slower we move the faster we die. Make no mistake, moving is living. Some animals were meant to carry each other to live symbiotically over a lifetime. Star-crossed lovers, monogamous swans. We are not swans. We are sharks."

Ryan is detached—and "not in no kinda good way."
    Many religions teach detachment (well, actually non-attchment and there *is* a difference) as way to achieve peace. Life is suffering. Suffering comes from attachment. End attachment, end suffering. But this practice isn't a defensive, closed position of self-preservation so much as an end to idolatry and a freedom from the prison of possessiveness. I try to practice it less as detachment from than as attachment to—to everything and everyone. Who is my neighbor? Everyone—particularly those in need.
    Jason Reitman has made a quiet, affecting adult film— sophisticated and thoughtful—so timely as to make one believe in stars aligning and synchronicity. And he cast his film to perfection.
    All of the actors in *Up in the Air* deliver brilliant performances,

particularly Vera Farmiga and Anna Kindrick, but even amidst a stellar cast, George Clooney's star shines so bright as to nearly eclipse the others.

Like a lot of movie stars, George Clooney, perhaps the closest thing to an old-fashioned, Cary Grantesque movie star we have, is never not himself on screen. We're not watching Ryan Bingham so much as George Clooney using the name Ryan Bingham. But of all the roles we've watched George Clooney play, this one seems to best suit his suave, charming coolness. In fact, characters don't come much cooler than Ryan Bingham—cool all the way down to his detached, cold core.

I hope you'll give *Up in the Air* a go. With open heart and mind, I hope you'll take it in and be challenged by it, for whether we are overattached or overly detached, we can learn much from Ryan Bingham—even if mostly it's how *not* to be.

Sense of Place

Great fiction is specific.

It's counterintuitive, but the more personal, more specific a piece of fiction is, the more universal its appeal. A big part of the authority of fiction (an absolute essential element for it to be effective) is the specificity required to make people and places come to life.

A sense of place is the conveyance of the quiddity of a geographic location—that which makes it unique, that which distinguishes it from other places and causes the people of that place to care for and be attached to it. It usually includes a set of personal, family, and community narratives that include features of the place, as well as the attribution of non-material characteristics to the place, which attempt to describe its soul.

If realism is an author's goal, a sense of place is the key to achieving it. By carefully and authentically capturing a place, an author not only conveys the specific regionalism required to sustain a fictive dream, but she also makes possible the credible characters who are so connected to that place that the two are inseparable.

When I left the theater after watching *The Town*, it occurred to me that Ben Affleck, not surprisingly, does his best work when he's working at home—in his own backyard, with his own kith and kin. The thing *Good Will Hunting*, *Gone Baby Gone*, and *The Town* have in common is a sense of place (and, therefore, of people)—Boston and all its complexities that Affleck understands like only a local can (he grew up in Cambridge).

Like Dennis Lehane, who writes about the area and who penned the novel *Gone Baby Gone*, Affleck brings a sense of gritty realism to his work set in Boston neighborhoods that give it a credibility that seems nearly non-fiction in nature.

The Town is an excellent movie, a thrilling, suspenseful character-driven drama of sympathetic characters in difficult and dangerous situations, mostly, though not entirely, of their own makings—they are, after all, products of this place they have such a sense of.

Doug MacRay (Ben Affleck) is an unrepentant criminal, the de facto leader of a group of ruthless bank robbers who pride themselves in stealing what they want and getting out clean. With no real attachments, Doug never has to fear losing anyone close to him. But that all changed on the gang's latest job, when they briefly took a hostage—bank manager Claire Keesey (Rebecca Hall). Though they let her go unharmed, Claire is nervously aware that the robbers know her name... and where she lives. But she lets her guard down when she meets an unassuming and rather charming man named Doug—not realizing that he is the same man who only days earlier had terrorized her. The instant attraction between them gradually turns into a passionate romance that threatens to take them both down a dangerous, and potentially deadly, path.

Affleck is both a talented actor and director—and to be able to do both so well simultaneously is truly extraordinary. As an actor, he brings out great performances from the actors he's directing—whether they are professionals or the locals he casts to give his films such a realistic sense of place.

To see Ben Affleck's evolution as an artist—both as an actor and director, see *Good Will Hunting* and *Gone Baby Gone*, and then *The Town*. It's the least expensive way to visit Boston—and arguably the way to have more interesting adventures than taking an actual, physical trip.

A Proposal of Love

Can love truly change a person?

Romance movies in general, and *The Proposal* in particular, beg the question.

(Before we go any further, I'd like to suggest that you listen to Tracy Chapman's song "Change" as you read—or at least when you finish reading.)

In *The Proposal*, Sandra Bullock plays high-powered book editor Margaret Tate, who is facing deportation back to Canada. The quick-thinking exec declares that she's actually engaged to her unsuspecting put-upon assistant, Andrew Paxton (played by Ryan Reynolds), who she's tormented for years.

He agrees to participate in the charade, but with a few conditions of his own. The unlikely couple heads to Alaska to meet his quirky family, and the always-in-control city girl finds herself in one comedic fish-out-of-water situation after another. With an impromptu wedding in the works and an immigration official on their heels, Margaret and Andrew reluctantly vow to stick to the plan despite the precarious consequences.

Sandra Bullock is a beautiful, charming, funny actress who has seldom found (or chosen) material equal to her abilities—and *The Proposal* is no different.

The movie's not bad as romantic comedies go, but it's not great, doesn't take advantage of many opportunities and situations, lacks chemistry, and never really gets going before it's over—though Betty White is a bright spot (as usual).

The premise of the *The Proposal* is that Andrew's and his family's love for Margaret (and her love for him and them) can change her.

It's a nice notion—one I happen to subscribe to, but not in a heady weekend-whirlwind-wedding way.

Romances claim that finding the right person and "falling" in love is life changing. They are often trite, cliché-ridden, and involve far more attraction and infatuation than actual love, but beneath their shallow surface and behind their enduring popularity is the notion that love changes things—and might just change everything.

Does love change a person? Does anything else?

Love changes us when we let it, when we open ourselves up to it, remove any blockages in our lives so that it might flow to and then through us.

I'm convinced love changes us—that nothing determines the people we are more than love or its absence. Not the "falling in love" of romances, which is, in part, the euphoria of illusion, but the unconditional love that comes from God—love as a choice, love as an experience, love as a lifestyle, love as a philosophy, love as a religion, love as compassion (feeling what others feel) that motivates us to extend ourselves on the behalf of others, love that, unlike "romantic love," which is all about attraction and desire (largely self-centered stuff), is not based on the beloved (his or her qualities, attractiveness, or worthiness).

There's a lot of wisdom in separating love from like, from desire and attraction and infatuation. There are so many things we call love that just aren't.

Love as illusion, as infatuation, as the projection of perfection onto a person can change us temporarily, but love as a choice made every moment, as an end of illusions, as an act of generosity, as accepting someone the way they are, has the greatest chance of changing us no less than those we love.

Love as a feeling fades (waxes and wanes, ebbs and flows). Love as a lifestyle, as a worldview, as a religion, as a commitment despite how we feel, grows, expands, engulfs.

In the simple and profound lyrics of Clint Black:

Love is certain, love is kind
Love is yours and love is mine
But it isn't something that we find
It's something that we do
We're on a road that has no end
And each day we begin again
Love's not just something that we're in
It's something that we do
There's no request too big or small
We give ourselves, we give our all
Love isn't someplace that we fall
It's something that we do

Clint is right. Love isn't a condition, it's an action. Love isn't something that happens to us, it's a lifestyle choice.

You could do worse for romantic comedy movie-time than spending it at *The Proposal*, but it's the film's implicit question that we should spend our time reflecting on, whether we see the movie or not.

I propose we commit ourselves to love—to embracing, accepting, and giving, to unconditionally extending ourselves on the behalf of others—not just those we're attracted to, or who are like us, but also, or especially, to those who don't love us back, to even our enemies, and see what happens. True change will occur—in us if no one else.

Kingdoms in Conflict

Leo Tolstoy said, "The kingdom of God is within you."
He wasn't the first to say it.

After penning what many believe to be two of the best novels ever written, *Anna Karenina* and *War and Peace*, he spent his later life studying and writing about the kingdom of God.

Jesus's teachings, encapsulated in the Sermon on the Mount, became the foundation upon which Tolstoy attempted to build his life and legacy.

The kingdom of God is within—not without. Not of institutions or empires, church or state, but of love.

It is not only opposite the world, but opposed to it—standing as an alternative, a current that is counter to culture and creed, dynasties and domination systems.

As such, the kingdom of God functions differently than the kingdom of the world. Those who live by it trust, share what they have, love everyone—even enemies—refuse to retaliate, and fight greed and hate, inequality, and injustice. In stark contrast, the world, fueled by selfishness and greed, is largely controlled by money and power, manipulation and physical force, oppression and brutality, most often putting the might of the majority in power over the rights of the multitudes.

The kingdom that's within rejects power, refuses to use physical force. Built on compassion and justice, it operates in freedom and love—which are virtually the same thing—making a priority of helping the poor, the oppressed, the least, the lowest, the marginalized and disenfranchised.

In Tolstoy's antiestablishment and antiauthoritarian *The Kingdom of God is Within You: Christianity Not as a Mystical Religion but as a New Theory of Life*, he argues that all societies contain social systems of wealth and power based on the inequitable distribution of wealth where, even as governments and ideologies change, domination systems use the threat of force to protect institutional inequality. The powerful maintain their power because of systemic oppression, and under the threat of force and the allure of material desire, individuals committed to maintaining the status quo are actually instruments of their own domination.

Power corrupts.

Like the Roman Empire Jesus challenged or the Russian Empire Tolstoy railed against, our culture is corrupt. Greed has led to a domination system that, through brainwashing of state and church and family, leads most of us to walk around in a hypnotic state, faithful cogs in the very machine that oppresses us.

But as evil as injustice, inequity, oppression, and domination are, Tolstoy, like Gandhi and MLK, follows Jesus in his insistence that force can never be a part of the kingdom of God, and strictly adheres to Jesus's prohibition of responding to evil with evil. Freedom is love is right. Force is evil is wrong.

Tolstoy's radical commitment to Jesus's teaching, particularly his insistence on nonviolence and ending greed by the sharing of one's possessions, led him to reject the ownership of private property and to sign away his copyrights to his works, which in turn caused an epic battle with his wife—the last year of which is dramatized in Michael Hoffman's *The Last Station*.

After almost fifty years of marriage, the Countess Sofya (Helen Mirren), Leo Tolstoy's (Christopher Plummer) devoted wife, passionate lover, muse and secretary—she's copied out *War and Peace* six times... by hand!—suddenly finds her entire world turned upside down. In the name of his newly created religion, the great Russian novelist has renounced his noble title, his property, and even his family in favor of poverty, vegetarianism, and even celibacy—after she's borne him thirteen children!

When Sofya then discovers that Tolstoy's trusted disciple, Chertkov (Paul Giamatti)—whom she despises—may have secretly convinced her husband to sign a new will, leaving the rights to his iconic novels to the Russian people rather than his own family, she is consumed by righteous outrage. This is the last straw. Using every bit of cunning, every trick of seduction in her considerable arsenal, she fights fiercely for what she believes is rightfully hers. The more extreme her behavior becomes, however, the more easily Chertkov is able to persuade Tolstoy of the damage she will do to his glorious legacy.

Into this minefield wanders Tolstoy's worshipful new assistant, the young, gullible Valentin (James McAvoy). In no time, he becomes a pawn, first of the scheming Chertkov and then of the wounded, vengeful Sofya as each plots to undermine the other's gains. Complicating Valentin's life even further is the overwhelming passion he feels for the beautiful, spirited Masha (Kerry Condon), a free-thinking adherent of Tolstoy's new religion, whose unconventional attitudes about sex and love both compel and confuse him. Infatuated with Tolstoy's notions of ideal love, but mystified by the Tolstoys' rich and turbulent marriage, Valentin is ill-equipped to deal with the complications of love in the real world.

A tale of two romances, one beginning, one near its end, *The Last Station* is a complex, funny, rich, and emotional story about the difficulty of living with love and the impossibility of living without it.

Kingdoms come into conflict in *The Last Station*—inside Tolstoy as much as without. Any attempt to live in allegiance to the kingdom within will inevitably lead to conflicts with other kingdoms—without and within.

Hoffman has made an exquisite film of relationships and rhetoric, of love—love of people, love of principles. It's the story of spirit and flesh, of noble ideals and small-souled self-interest, all swirling around a gifted writer and thinker, a man attempting to live according to his convictions—no matter the cost.

Every element of the film works, but the directing and acting—particularly Plummer, Mirren, and Giamatti—are stunning.

Though only covering the last year of his life, *The Last Station* gives us a fascinating glimpse at Tolstoy and his struggles to follow Jesus.

Like Tolstoy, I attempt (and continually fail) to follow the true, simple, profound teachings of Jesus, to live according to the kingdom within, and, like him, this leads me to reject cultural status quo and the roles church and state, money and power, play in the domination system. I part company with Tolstoy when it comes to celibacy, but he did, too, until late in life. Perhaps I'll feel differently in my eighties (though I sincerely hope not). I also think there are ways to integrate the radical teachings of love and freedom, of nonattachment and nonviolence in everyday life, to be countercultural within one's own culture—as opposed to removing oneself completely from culture.

I recommend in addition to watching *The Last Station*, you also read *The Kingdom of God is Within You*, and in the process, search yourself, as Tolstoy did, for the kingdom of God inside you.

Definitely. Maybe. Definitely.

Finding a good romantic comedy is nearly as difficult as finding true love. It can be done, but not without some effort. You'll likely kiss a lot of frogs like Nicholas Sparks before you find a true prince like Richard Curtis.

Did I say Richard Curtis was a prince? My bad. I meant he's a king. Romantic comedies don't get any better than *Four Weddings and a Funeral*, *Notting Hill*, and *Love Actually*. But some get closer than others. The best I've seen in recent memory is *Definitely, Maybe*.

Definitely, Maybe is smart, funny, modern, mature, and even somewhat sophisticated for a romantic comedy (which I realize is like saying someone looks good for their age, but...).

The film is well written; the directing is good; Ryan Reynolds and Abigail Breslin are just fine; but what really elevates it are the powerhouse performances by its three leading ladies, Elizabeth Banks, Isla Fisher, and Rachel Weisz. They're all amazing, but Weisz is particularly beguiling, and Fisher is absolute perfection. In fact, I find Isla Fisher so irresistibly appealing I actually went to see *Confessions of a Shopaholic*. Hey, I'm not proud of it, but there it is—and she's worth the embarrassment.

Will Hayes has just received divorce papers from his wife at his advertising office in New York City. He picks up his eleven-year-old daughter, Maya, at school where she has just been taught sex education. Will can't take these new sex questions that Maya is asking, so agrees to tell her the story about how he met her mother. Will decides to tell Maya a bedtime story in the form of a puzzle with the names changed so she must figure out which of the three loves of his life became his wife and her mother.

There are so many things to love about this movie—as I've said, its leading ladies chief among them. I love Will's idealism. I love the film's use of the time period to tether it to realism. Speaking of realism, I love the maturity and modernity of the adult relationships. And, of course, the relationship between dad and daughter—Will's Maya, like my Meleah (and all our children) are truly the happy endings of all our relationships.

I love to lose myself in a good romance, but I'm of two minds about them. Sometimes I think they are, as others have suggested, a kind of secular scripture, reminding us of the supremacy and life-altering power of love. Others, I fear, the very notion of the more shallow side of romantic love sets up unrealistic expectations and prevents many of us from ever finding the deep-abiding God-is-love kind of love that is beyond the heady-hysteria I-love-you-so-much-it's-retarded kind of romantic love. When the latter leads us to the former, infatuation can be a path to the divine, but if we spend a lifetime chasing the feelings the first blush of desire produces, we might completely miss the far more profound, abiding, selfless love we were each created to give and receive.

Definitely, Maybe is a good romantic comedy. Is it great? Can it join the company of *Notting Hill* and *Love Actually*? Definitely. Maybe. Definitely. Maybe.

Find a Chair and Get in Treatment

It's not TV.

It's not.

Well, technically it is, but it's so far and away better than most of the drivel that's broadcast other places, it's like it's not even the same thing. In that way, it's like religion. You don't have to look very far to find two people who practice the same religion, yet one is consumed with hate, judgement, self-righteousness, fear, phobia, and is absolutely closed and defensive, while the other is consumed with compassion, filled with peace, fighting for an end to injustice and oppression, and is open and humble. They both may call themselves Christian or Jew or Muslim of Sikh, but they are not the same.

I said all that to say this: when they say, "It's not TV. It's HBO," though technically wrong, they are nonetheless accurate.

I've been a fan and faithful viewer of HBO's original series for quite a while now, going all the way back to my favorite New York girls, Carrie, Miranda, Charlotte, and Samantha. I also enjoyed spending time with the Fisher family, visiting Seth Bullock and his foulmouthed frenemies, and even to a lesser extent enjoy Sookie Stackhouse in spite of the actress's truly atrocious accent.

Now that *Sex and the City*, *Six Feet Under*, and *Deadwood* have gone the way of all flesh and other great shows like *Buffy* and *Gilmore*

Girls, I find that my favorite show next to *House* these days is *In Treatment*.

Flawed and fragile, Paul Weston is a wise, insightful, patient counselor, and a session with him is as therapeutic as any on TV. In the best tradition of wounded healers, he's a broken man in crisis, ministering out of his need—"Look at my hands and feet. It is I. Touch me and see."

That Paul is also in treatment, that the counselor becomes the counseled, gives the show a whole other dimension, showing us, therapy voyeurs, another side of him—a vulnerable and neurotic side his patients never see. After all, the man behind the curtain, the one we're supposed to pay no attention to, is always more interesting than anything else.

Shakespeare did it first, then much later, Hemingway reminded us. In the right hands, unalloyed dialog can be downright devastating—dramatic, suspenseful, intense, and interesting.

Conversation. Two people in a room talking. And it's as riveting as anything on TV.

In Treatment is worth paying the extra bucks to get HBO. It's the best value on my outrageous cable bill. Paul's patients are so sad and beautiful in their fractured humanity, in their longing (ultimately for love, though they may not know it), in their need for help to pick up the pieces and put them somehow back together again. Do you recognize them? They are lonely singles. They are miserable marrieds. They are sick and hurting. They are in crises. They are reevaluating. They are me. They are you.

I believe in counseling, have done a good bit of it over the years—both inside prison and out—and have so many intimates who are counselors, that I feel like I've been in treatment my entire adult life. Few things are better for us, more therapeutic, than a safe, nonjudgmental place where we can say absolutely anything we need to, where we can bring forth the monsters in our minds and, in the light of love and understanding, see how very small they really are. Is there anything we humans need more than to be heard and understood? That's why the art of counseling, like the art of friendship, is mostly about listening. Sure, an occasional question or insight is helpful, but nothing compares to being heard and accepted, and knowing what we say will be taken to the grave.

Some of the best counseling I've received over the years has come from books by or about counselors—particularly the gentle, tender, Thomas Moore, who truly does the work of caring for the soul. It was he who taught me that our word *therapy* has *chair* in its etymology, and how very appropriate that is, how very Zen ("when sitting, just sit"). In this, to sit with someone, to share their burden is to care for their soul, is to give them counsel and treatment. It's something we can all do for each other—and something Paul Weston is doing for me each week in our sessions on Sunday and Monday nights. Feel free to join us.

Continental Divide

Shakespeare rightly noted, "The course of true love never did run smooth."

This is particularly true of the love found in romance fiction where the genre convention is to introduce two potential lovers with enormous chemistry and desire then place as many obstacles between them as possible.

Obstacles to love are too numerous to name, but they're dwindling. No longer are class, race, sex credible impediments. Part of the reason *Notting Hill* works so well is that fame as a hindrance in our celebrity-obsessed culture is so believable. And with *Going the Distance* we have another. The world is shrinking to be sure, but not enough to solve the enormous issues of a bicoastal relationship.

Drew Barrymore and Justin Long star in this romantic comedy about a long-distance romance that may be worth fighting for. Garrett (Long) is still nursing the wounds from a recent breakup when he meets Erin (Barrymore), an unflinchingly honest girl with a big talent for bar trivia. Hitting it off immediately, the pair spend a romantic summer together in New York City. It was supposed to be a summer fling, but as fall approaches and Erin returns to San Francisco, the spark is still there. Subsequently dividing his days between working and hitting the bars with best friends Box (Jason Sudeikis) and Dan (Charlie Day), Garrett drops everything whenever Erin calls. The more Garrett's phone rings, the more his pals begin to suspect that their drinking buddy is taking the relationship a little too seriously. And they're not the only ones; Erin's sister, Corrine (Christina Applegate), is keen to ensure that her smitten sibling doesn't repeat the mistakes of her past, and she makes no attempts to sugarcoat the fact that she disapproves of the coast-to-coast romance. But the heart wants what the heart wants, and as the texting becomes more intense, both Garrett and Erin start to suspect that their summer fling may just be the real thing.

Going the Distance is a stellar romantic comedy—genuine and genuinely funny. Its honest, real, credible look at the issues of long-distance dating never feel false or forced. The film never overreaches in the way so many do, never gives us unearned emotion or over-the-top, melodramatic plot twists. It's a comedy about adults for adults, with mature, often sexual, humor that rises organically out of who the characters are, their relationship, and the situation they find themselves in.

Barrymore is, as usual, adorable, and she and Long make a sweet, convincing couple in a relationship worth working out. Speaking of working…the chosen professions of the couple (print journalist and music promoter) not only provide authentic challenges and obstacles, but reflect the upheaval both industries are experiencing right now.

Going the Distance works so well, is so good, that it is easily the most fun, enjoyable experience I've had in a movie theater in a very long time, and I can already hear the film knocking on the door of my top-ten romcom list. It's the kind of romantic comedy you can give yourself over to and not regret it the morning after.

You Make My Heart Sing

I've never cared much for kid movies. The ones I've endured, I've done so for my children, and even at a young age, they picked up on the fact that Dad spent a good deal of time in the lobby during the feature presentation.

Over the years, I've been subjected to Power Rangers, Pokemon, a pig named Babe, and dozens of Disney animated fairytales because they're what my children wanted to watch, but recently, with a little time on my hands following a book signing, I went to the theater right by myself and watched *Where the Wild Things Are*.

I didn't do it for my children, but the child in me.

Where the Wild Things Are is an adaptation of Maurice Sendak's classic children's story, where Max, a disobedient little boy sent to bed without his supper, creates his own world—a forest inhabited by ferocious wild creatures that crown Max as their ruler.

I've done a bit of adaptation—both of my own work and that of others—and know just how difficult it is to translate a work of art into another medium. There's a real art to it—an art on brilliant and beautiful display in Spike Jonze's and Dave Eggars' work here. They have taken the ten sentences of Sendak's beloved book and created a psychologically sophisticated and emotionally resonate film.

With an economy of words and some wonderful images, the

book allows us to project our own particular wildness into the story (like all good stories do), to use our imaginations to fill in the spaces, to cast ourselves in the role of Max or one of the monsters, but the film largely does this for us, fleshing out characters and relationships and events, leaving few narrative gaps.

Some say music sooths the savage beast, and it's true, but Max shows that story is far more effective. With childlike abandon, he spins tales that mesmerize the monsters. In fact, the power of story is one of the most significant and profound themes of the film. The entire work is a story, of course, but then there's the story Max overhears his mom telling on the telephone, the story he tells her later as he's settling in for bed, and the story he tells himself—the one that is his entire adventure. Story allows us to safely explore our wild sides, it comforts and heals and helps us make sense of the world. Our imaginations really are the most wondrous and wild things of all.

Max discovers much during his wild adventure—experiencing the pain of separation, the grief of loss, the solitude of leadership— but nothing he learns is more important or profound than the fact that even (or especially) Wild Things need mothers. As king, Max realizes just how difficult it is to be a parent—and how lucky he is to have one. In fact, the only thing keeping Max from complete anarchy, from being as lost and as damaged as the Wild Things, is his mom. With a loving mother, a little Wild Thing can be a caring leader. Without a positive maternal influence, Wild Things too quickly become monsters that smash and destroy. We, like Max, need a mom—and not just in personal, but in public life. Our country and the world would be better if our sexist, male-dominated culture would make room for Mother (Mother God, Mother Earth, Yin, a celebrated and appreciated public feminine presence) and wouldn't attempt to force a type of masculinity on women in positions of authority and leadership.

The Wild Things in Max's mind (actual facets of Max's personality) continually do damage. There's a good deal of destruction in the film—particularly by Max and Carol—and it comes from their inability to deal with the strong emotions they experience. In Max and his Wild Things, we finally have a kid in film who is fully formed— untamed and unpredictable, resilient and vulnerable, wild, yet ultimately domesticated.

Where are the Wild Things? Inside us as much as Max, and, like Max, we need to let them out occasionally so they can run and roar.

Sure, this can be done literally—plenty of people out there howling at the moon every night—but there are endless ways to take a walk on the wild side, including and especially art, and you could do far worse than reading or seeing *Where The Wild Things Are*. Figurative destruction is almost always better than actual, but a little wildness and even demolition all along is better than the catastrophic kind that inevitably explodes out of repression. What I'm saying is there's a beast beneath our breast, and we need to let it out to breathe occasionally. So now, let the wild rumpus start.

For Lovers Only

In the final analysis, love is not only all that matters, it's all there is.

Lovers understand this better than anyone.

In love, we are given opportunity to glimpse God, to experience eternity, to know true oneness.

"Just as in earthly life lovers long for the moment when they are able to breathe forth their love for each other, to let their souls blend in a soft whisper," wrote Soren Kierkegaard, "so the mystic longs for the moment when in prayer he can, as it were, creep into God."

In love, duality disappears. There is no separation, no me and you, I and thou, no distance. The veil rends and there is only love.

In love, the world wanes away and lovers dissolve into divinity.

In love, there is only gratitude.

As Ralph W. Stockman put it, "A true lover always feels in debt to the one he loves."

Capturing love, which, it can be argued, is why art was invented, is never easy, but most romances show two people falling in love—finding each other, becoming attracted, then infatuated, and ultimately falling for one another only to face obstacles and impediments.

For Lovers Only captures *being* in love—being beautifully, heartbreakingly, exquisitely in love.

It's a romance directed by Michael Polish and written by Mark Polish, starring Stana Katic and Mark Polish.

In the film, Katic plays Sofia, a journalist and former model, while Polish plays Yves, a former fashion photographer. Sofia chances upon Yves, a former lover, while on assignment. The story draws upon Claude Lelouch's *A Man and a Woman* and the French New Wave for inspiration and focuses on the couple's flight from Paris via a variety of forms of transportation: train, car, and motorcycle. Their travels extend from Normandy to St. Tropez. Mark Polish notes that the film lies somewhere between *A Man and a Woman* and the Beatles' *A Hard Day's Night*. The film was shot in Paris and various locations throughout Europe.

For Lovers Only is a photographic work of art. Shot in black and white, each frame looks like classic photography, which not only shows just how remarkably beautiful Stana Katic really is, but also enhances the enchanted entanglements of the two lovers. In artistic black and white, "in love" looks like what it is—a heightened, sensual, hyper-reality of blissful, ecstatic, peace.

All these achievements are not to say that the film is flawless. The sound quality is poor, the soundtrack sometimes jarring, and there's a general lack of coherence that culminates in an unearned and, for the most part, unexplained ending.

Still, for a heady, erotic, ecstatic, romantic romp that convincingly captures what being in love is like, I highly recommend *For Lovers Only*.

The Quiet American

The American is a quiet little film, visually arresting, slowly affecting—a well-crafted work of art, but on the artisan more than artist end of the artistic spectrum.

At one point, an insightful and observant priest notes that the main character, who presents himself as a photographer, has the hands of a craftsman more than an artist. It's hard to think of a better way to describe the film itself. Well built. Beautiful. Work of craftsmanship. Not an artistic masterpiece.

Academy Award winner George Clooney stars in the title role of this suspense thriller. As an assassin, Jack (Clooney) is constantly on the move and always alone. After a job in Sweden ends more harshly than expected for this American abroad, Jack retreats to the Italian countryside. He relishes being away from death for a spell as he holes up in a small medieval town. While there, Jack takes an assignment to construct a weapon for a mysterious contact, Mathilde (Thekla Reuten). Savoring the peaceful quietude he finds in the mountains of Abruzzo, Jack accepts the friendship of local priest Father Benedetto (Paolo Bonacelli) and pursues a relationship with a beautiful prostitute named Clara (Violante Placido). Jack and Clara's time together seems hopeful and free of danger, but is such a thing possible for a man like Jack?

The American was written by Rowan Joffe, based on the novel

A Very Private Gentleman, by Martin Booth, and directed by Anton Corbijn, a Dutch photographer who has worked extensively in the music industry. His feature film debut was *Control*, a film about the life of Joy Division frontman Ian Curtis.

Cinematography is often referred to as painting with light or writing with light, which is exactly what Corbijn does so brilliantly. Every frame of the film is picturesque—carefully composed, exquisitely captured. In this age of digital video, in the era when film is supposedly "dead," it's good to imagine holding up a strip of film to the light and considering how each frame is a still photograph. Corbijn's work is a good reminder, and it makes me think that a photographer making a movie is like a poet writing a novel—any sacrifice in narrative drive is often made up for by beauty, artistry, and craftsmanship.

Like the film itself, Clooney's performance is stripped down. Quiet. Sparse. Spartan. There's none of the usual Clooney charm, and the movie is the better for it. Also like the film, Violante Placido is breathtakingly beautiful, her body carefully crafted by a true artist, every shot of her a photograph worth framing and hanging. Equally as beautiful, though in a very different way, is the conscience of this well-crafted film—Father Benedetto, played brilliantly by Paolo Bonacelli. He provides humble, helpful insight, wisdom, and service, an egoless spiritual caretaker worthy of confessing to.

If over-the-top, cartoonish Hollywood action-adventure movies have left you unsatisfied, try this art-house thriller. The quiet ride it provides is far more effective, far more enthralling, far more resonate than big-budget bombs and one-dimensional good and bad guys could ever be.

Paper and Fire

Charlyne Yi doesn't believe in love. Or so she says. Though she never says it explicitly, it's probably more accurate to say that she doesn't believe in fairy-tale, romantic "love."

Paper Heart follows Charlyne as she embarks on a quest across America to make a documentary about this subject she doesn't understand. As she and her good friend (and director) Nick search for answers and advice about love, Charlyne talks with friends and strangers, scientists, bikers, romance novelists, and children. They each offer diverse views on modern romance, as well as various answers to the age-old question: does true love really exist?

Then, shortly after filming begins, Charlyne meets a boy after her own heart—Michael Cera (the actor from *Juno* and *Nick and Nora's Infinite Playlist*). Combining elements of documentary and traditional storytelling, reality, and fantasy, *Paper Heart* brings a unique perspective to romantic comedies; however, I suspect there's far more fiction in this film than there appears to be.

Paper Heart so combines reality and fantasy, so blurs the lines between the two, it's best not to take anything in it too seriously. Still, it is, nonetheless, thought-provoking.

I found watching *Paper Heart* odd and interesting because Charlyne Yi doesn't believe in love, and there's nothing I believe in more.

Of course, that's not exactly what I mean. Belief is cheap. Easy. Shallow. Practice is the thing. As a philosophy, a religion, a way of being in the world, I attempt to practice love. I'm committed to it.

There's nothing more central to my existence than love, and there I was sitting in the old AMC theater in the Panama City Mall, where back in the day I went on my first movie date, watching a film about a person who claims not to believe in love.

Throughout the film, on a road trip of sorts, Charlyne asks people what love is, and it's interesting to see people grapple to define love—and to hear how different their definitions are from one another.

I sympathize. Love is difficult to define. But this is how it should be. Defining something limits it (which is why it's best not to do it, or when we do, leave an opening). Love can't be limited. It must be free. Love and freedom are inseparable. How can we define something that is bigger than and, in many ways, beyond us, *and* must be free?

The longer I watched the movie, the more I realized that Charlyne, the girl who doesn't believe in love, and me, the boy who believes in it more than anything, are actually much more closely aligned than it would first appear.

When Charlyne claims not to believe in love, she actually means romantic, lightning-bolt, head-over-heels infatuation where the object of our desire and affection becomes the god of our idolatry and that this is *true* love. But this isn't love at all. Sure, it's been known to lead to love, but more often than not it leads to disillusionment. Why? Because it's an illusion—a projection onto a person of what we want and need. It's a fantasy. Love is a reality.

Don't get me wrong, I fall in infatuation all the time. It's a heady and happy experience, and I even refer to it in the popular parlance as "falling in love," but I know enough to know it ain't love. It's like. It's desire. It's attraction. It's fire. It's not love.

What is love then? I'll happily give you one of my definitions if you promise to leave it open so it can be free.

Love is the uncoerced and unconditional commitment to continually accept and extend as a response to love itself.

God is love. Love is God. Love flows to us, then through us. We are responding to love by loving God back, genuinely and without ego loving ourselves, and loving all others as ourselves.

Is my definition wanting? Of course. Any and all definitions of love are. It's the same with God (a coincidence? I think not).

Love is universal. It can't be limited to one person, one family, one tribe, one race, one nationality, or only to those who love us. Sure, people do it, and even call it love, but it's not. If I "love" only "my" children, it's not love. If I "love" only "my" parents, it's not love. Who are my children, my parents, my brothers, my sisters, my wives, my husbands, my neighbors? Everyone. Or no one.

Does Charlyne find love? Does she discover what it really is? You'll have to watch it to find out. But you don't have to wait any time at all to be loved and to love. You, like Charlyne and me, are loved. We just are—nothing we can do about it—and what we do with that unconditional acceptance determines the quality of our lives and the good we do in the world more than anything else. By far.

Whether we have a paper heart or an organ of fire, we are loved and meant to love—not in word only, but in deed. After all, love is not a condition, but an action—a verb, not a noun.

If you, like Charlyne, are not sure you believe in love—or even know what it is, just try this: Open yourself up to it, to how accepted, valued, cherished you are, and then commit to love as a way of life, begin to accept others (no longer judging or condemning), extend yourself for them, do, to the best of your ability, what is best for them, and see what happens.

1 in 29,000

One day.

One among many.

If you and I reach current life expectancies, we'll have nearly twenty-nine thousand days.

And though no two will be exactly alike, some will be far more unalike than others.

Some will be magic. Perfect. Extraordinary.

Certain days will be so incredible we can't imagine any way they could be any better.

Then there will be those that we can't imagine being any worse.

Of course, the truth is our lives are made of moments more than days—and what we're recalling about our best and worst days are actually certain moments within them.

The moments of our lives are as mysterious as life itself.

Why, against all odds, do some people become lifelong friends and others drift away on the currents of existence, scarcely to be recalled?

Why do some friends become lovers? Why do some lovers become enemies?

And how can it be that we can crisscross paths with soul mates before finally finding one another, finally accepting a fate so sweet only heaven could create it after twenty years? Thirty? Forty?

It's rare, but it happens—and not just in romance novels and the movies made from them.

Life is far more mysterious than we realize—"There are more things in heaven and earth, Horatio, Than are dreamt of in your philosophy"—and our attempts at narrative and structure, explanation and meaning are fragile attempts at reassurance, facades propped up to the illusion of control and the denial of chaos. But the narrative of life is far more like that of dreams than causally connected story.

Moment by moment, day by day, magic happens. And sometimes, just sometimes, we perceive it.

Twenty years. Two people…

After one day together—July 15, 1988, their college graduation—Emma Morley (Academy Award nominee Anne Hathaway) and Dexter Mayhew (Jim Sturgess of *Across the Universe*) begin a friendship that will last a lifetime. She is a working-class girl of principle and ambition who dreams of making the world a better place. He is a wealthy charmer who dreams that the world will be his playground.

For the next two decades, key moments of their relationship are experienced over several July fifteenths in their lives. Together and apart, we see Dex and Em through their friendship and fights, hopes and missed opportunities, laughter and tears. Somewhere along their journey, these two people realize that what they are searching and hoping for has been there for them all along. As the true meaning of that one day back in 1988 is revealed, they come to terms with the nature of love and life itself.

Directed by Lone Scherfig (director of *An Education*, Academy Award-nominated for Best Picture), the motion picture *One Day* is adapted for the screen by David Nicholls from his beloved bestselling novel *One Day*.

I went to the theater to see *One Day* the movie while in the middle of reading *One Day* the book, which is almost always a horrible, terrible thing to do, but it is a testament to just how well made the movie is that I liked it—liked it a lot—in spite of it being so much less than the book. Scherfig has crafted a fine film—gorgeous and moving with terrific performances all-round.

The plot of both the book and movie is predictable but forgivable because of the execution of the writing and storytelling, the depth, roundedness, and chemistry of the characters, and the skill and vividness with which each era is captured.

I suggest reading the book and seeing the movie—and using both as a reminder of how precious every day, every moment, is.

Each moment of our lives has the potential to be magic, to be a key moment, if we'll open ourselves to the mystery. In the final analysis all moments are important, vital, fraught with opportunity, each a gift awaiting unwrapping.

Ultimately, all we ever have is one day. It's always the day after yesterday. Always. Just today. There is no day before and tomorrow never ever arrives. Live this one day like it's your only one—because it is.

Chaos and Creativity

The act of creation is often chaotic.

As Marilyn Ferguson said, "The creative process requires chaos before form emerges."

Artists work with chaos—a truth embodied in Sharon Hubbard's observation that "the creation of true art requires some mysterious innate ability to thrive in chaos."

Art is an attempt at creating order out of chaos—or at the very least a way of searching for and assigning meaning to the chaos itself.

There's a random, mysterious, sometimes chaotic element to the universe that I think those of us who spend our time engaged in creating art are particularly sensitive to. Perhaps that's why chaos theory so appeals to me, and why one of my favorite sayings is, "God created order out of chaos, but sometimes the chaos shows through." This is also why, for me, any religion, philosophy, or worldview that claims to explain everything is simplistic, shortsighted, and suspect (seriously lacking in credibility).

In dealing with the chaos of existence, there seem to be two approaches—those of us who welcome, even invite, it in, and those who attempt, with all the defensiveness they can muster, to keep it at bay.

My own approach is one of openness—honoring the random, the chaotic, the humbling that reminds me just how not in control I really am—all the while careful to avoid manufactured drama and the destructiveness of unnecessary anarchy. But regardless of the approach, the artist and spiritually open person can't afford not to embrace the whirlwind.

Like everything else, there are counterfeits for chaos, and some people get addicted to the rush and so continually create circumstances so that their lives resemble a Tilt-A-Whirl ride. Some artists suck on chaos like it's a crack pipe, and so recklessly and routinely set fire to their own lives.

Guido Contini, whose story is told in Rob Marshall's musical, *Nine*, appears to be just such an artist—a gifted writer/director who's lost all control of his life and appetites. In fact, at one point his estranged wife, Luisa, tells him that that's all he is—an appetite.

Guido Contini (Daniel Day-Lewis), famous Italian film director, has turned forty and faces a double crisis: he has to shoot a film for which he can't write the script; and his wife of twenty years, the film star Luisa del Forno (Marion Cotillard), may be about to leave him. As it turns out, it is the same crisis.

Luisa's efforts to talk to him seem to be drowned out by voices in his head—voices of women in his life, speaking through the walls of his memory, insistent, flirtatious, irresistible, potent. Women Guido has loved, and from whom he has derived the entire vitality of a creative life, now as stalled as his marriage—his mistress (Penelope Cruz), his film star muse (Nicole Kidman), his confidant and costume designer (Judi Dench), an American fashion journalist (Kate Hudson), the prostitute from his youth (Fergie), and his mother (Sophia Loren).

As Guido struggles to find a story for his film, he becomes increasingly preoccupied—his interior world sometimes becoming indistinguishable from the objective world—and his producer suggests he make a musical, an idea which itself veers off into a feminine fantasy of extraordinary vividness.

Nine is the film adaptation of a musical inspired by Fellini's mesmerizing classic, *8 1/2*. Ordinarily, I'm not much on musicals, but because of the subject matter here and its connection to Fellini and *8 1/2*, I wanted to see *Nine* from the moment I heard about it. And the film did not disappoint. I expected to like the story in spite of the musical intrusions, but found myself really responding to a few of the numbers, and appreciating the masterful way Marshall stitched them into the seam of the narrative. I really enjoyed the musical performance by Fergie, which is not surprising, but what I found shocking was just how talented a singer Kate Hudson is. But it's not the musical but the dramatic performances that make the movie something special, and though all are particularly strong, Daniel Day-Lewis is again amazing, and Marion Cotillard is absolutely heartbreaking.

Being creative involves chaos. But nothing is as chaotic as the frustration that results from the chaos in an artist's life becoming so out of balance that it no longer allows for creativity. Few films embody these truths as dramatically and powerfully as *8 1/2* and *Nine*.

Saul Bellow said that "art is the achievement of stillness in the midst of chaos"—something Guido has yet to learn.

In life, as in art, there's real skill involved in managing chaos. Of course, chaos can't be controlled. I'm not suggesting it can. Maybe it can't even be managed, but *we* can. We can manage ourselves, our responses.

Maybe managing chaos is like trying to make a movie without a script, or maybe it's an altogether absurd notion in the way "talking about love is like dancing about architecture." And in the end, that's what *8 1/2* and *Nine* and life are all about—love. Love that drives us to create. Create connections—with our words, our bodies, our beings, our art—and, in doing so, touch the void, approach the whirlwind, open our belts and minds and hearts to chaos. A chaos that, depending on how we respond, can lead to creation or destruction—to art, to a more artful life, or to even more chaos.

Jill and Kevin's Infinite Entrance

Some people just know how to make an entrance.

Jill and Kevin do.

If you haven't seen their wedding entrance, you should. Go to YouTube to view it and become part of the phenomenon.

I've watched it a dozen times already—and each and every one I laugh and I cry simultaneously.

Why have over eleven million people watched Jill and Kevin and their wedding party march down the aisle? Why have I (and so many others) watched it over and over again? Why did it bring a smile to my face even as it brought tears to my eyes?

Perhaps partly because the best things online, from how-to videos to advice columns, from parodies to porn, involve amateurs—DIYs, poets, independent artists, and stay-at-home moms who now have a means to share their ideas, their work, themselves.

Professionals do it for money, but amateurs do it for love.

A professional is someone who makes a living doing what they do; an amateur is someone who loves it so much they live to do it.

As a writer, I've always attempted to be a professional-amateur—striving for the skill, knowledge, expertise, and experience of a professional, yet having love as my primary if not only motivation. I write because I love to, and I write about what I love (and I love Jill and

Kevin and their friends!).

There's not a professional dancer among them, and there
are only a few decent ones. And that's what makes it so moving, so
powerful, such a YouTube phenomenon.

We'd expect to see art students or professional performers
dance their way down the aisle of a nonreligious venue they were getting
married in, but for average Jills and Joes to dance down the aisle of a
church as part of what looks to be a fairly traditional wedding—it's not
just unexpected, it's refreshingly authentic.

Give me genuine actions over polished performances any day.

But that's only part of the reason this five-minute video has
become the most popular clip flying through cyber space at the moment.

Another reason? Friends.

Having friends to stand with us during the momentous or
difficult days of our lives is something we all deeply and desperately
need (and increasingly don't have), but to have ones who will dance with
us—what could be better? What is a friend after all, but someone who
cares enough for us to weep when we weep, dance when we dance?

I try to be the kind of friend who will gladly dance down the
aisle of life with others, and am constantly looking for friends who will
do the same. They are not easy to find—Jill and Kevin are truly blessed.

I suspect yet another reason the video has become so popular is
the song.

Let me be clear, I don't think a woman should be with a man
who hits her—not even one time (and it's never just one time), and I
will not be buying any more of Chris Brown's music. A man who would
beat a woman—any person who would use their relative power, be it
physical or otherwise to impose his or her will, has lost the best part
of their humanity and needs treatment, not a world tour. That said,
art transcends the artist in the way truth transcends the flawed vessel
it's poured through, and the song was an excellent choice for a young
couple dancing down the aisle together.

> It's you and me moving
> At the speed of light into eternity yea
> Tonight is the night to join me in the middle of ecstasy
> Feel the melody in the rhythm of the music around you
> (around you)

It's like I've waited my whole life for this one night
It's gonna be me, you, and the dance floor
'Cause we've only got one night (one night)
Double your pleasure
Double your fun and dance
Forever (ever, ever)

Some people really do seem to see marriage as the "one night" they wait their whole lives for—anticipate, long for, feel less than without. And though marriage began as a sexist institution for men to protect their property (which included their wives) and has become a prison of culture and a weapon of exclusion, it's still possible for good, healthy, relationships to exist within it in spite of all this, in the same way humble, honorable, compassionate, there-for-the-right-reasons people are present in the flawed and broken institutions of religion. I hope Jill and Kevin have an empowering union that supports each of them in becoming their best selves. They appear to be off to a good start.

Finally, I think the video has become so popular because it involves dancing.

Dancing does something for our species that nothing else can. It's primal and comes from the deep soul, and in the industrialized, postmodern West, we don't do it enough. Sure we have dance as seduction, as sex with clothes on, and there's certainly a place for that. We have *Dancing with the Stars* and overly choreographed, overly structured dancing in certain places at certain times. We have dancing for others—demonstrating moves to impress or woo, but what about just dancing to dance—dancing because we are alive and few things feel as alive as feeling rhythm in our souls and expressing it through our bodies. Losing ourselves in something as spiritual and magical as music and dance is truly transcendent. But that's the key—losing that sense of self (and the self-consciousness it causes) in becoming one with the beat, the group, the world. Kevin and Jill and their friends may have been self-conscious and part of what they were doing may have had elements of performance, but most of it appears to be pure joy, caught up in the moment, being a good friend, being a—just being.

When I dance, which is often and often alone, it's because I'm experiencing something I can't contain, and when I do, I join the rocking rhythm of the undulating universe, whose strings are in constant creative motion, and in some mysterious way I'm joining all dancers—from

King David of Israel, to Michael Jackson, to ancient indigenous tribes in Africa, to as beautiful a bride as there has ever been, Jill, in a cosmic chorus that is primal, communal, sacred. Why not join us? At this very moment life is saying to you, May I have this dance?

A Maddening Silence

Increasingly, we're living in a world where nobody listens.

There's so much noise, such a continuous assault on our senses, that we have to create filters just to survive—but sometimes we filter out too much. Sometimes, we're not really listening to the important things being said and not being said to us.

It's as if we have an inverse form of ADHD—instead of letting everything in equally, we've stopped letting in much of anything at all. Of course, this is due in part to the rampant narcissism and self-involvement of our time, but I really do believe the deafening levels of noise, the sheer volume of stimuli have overwhelmed us to the point of living defensively—like little monkeys with our hands over our eyes and ears and minds.

Not so in the era of AMC's *Mad Men*, when television was still novel (on for only a few hours a day), people read, and the assault known as advertising and entertainment wasn't nearly so ubiquitous.

There is much to recommend about *Mad Men*—the characters, the sets, the sleek sexiness, but perhaps what is best about it is not what's in it, but what's left out.

The makers of *Mad Men* have mastered the art of silences.

Like the white space on a page of text, and the way it shapes the reading experience, the well-placed silences in *Mad Men* are exquisite and excruciating.

And it's not just the silences, but the overall quietness of the sophisticated drama. There's very little music, very little noise, just people talking—and not—so much so that commercial breaks are even more jarring in their intrusion than usual.

Set in 1960s New York, the sexy, stylized drama follows the lives of the men and women of Madison Avenue advertising. The series revolves around the conflicted Don Draper, the biggest ad man (and ladies' man) in the business, and his colleagues at the Sterling Cooper Advertising Agency. As Don makes the plays in the boardroom and the bedroom, he struggles to stay a step ahead of the rapidly changing times and the young executives nipping at his heels. The series also authentically depicts the roles of men and women in this era while exploring the true human nature beneath the guise of 1960s traditional family values.

Mad Men is one of the most existential dramas to ever air on TV. All the characters are vaguely aware something is missing, something isn't right, but for Don the feeling is anxiety-causing acute. We are given a front row seat to the lives of men and women trudging around the abyss, the quietness of their lives, the many silences around them, an outward manifestation of the noiseless void inside of them.

Relish the quiet and silence of *Mad Men*, get caught up in the spectacular set pieces and the turbulent times, and, most of all, the complex characters. As you do, remember, if it appears nothing is happening, look again. It's all there—only it's in the subtext. If you only hear the text, you'll miss it. If you only see what's on the surface, you won't perceive most of what's happening—the bulk of the berg moving these people is below the surface. Way below—where the current actually runs in a different direction.

If you haven't tried *Mad Men* or tried it and weren't immediately smitten, try it again. Still yourself from the frenzy of twenty-first century America's frantic pace, shut out the din and noise and sound and fury that is modern, manic, shallow culture, and embrace the essential silence at the heart of *Man Men*. Listen. It is the center of Job's whirlwind, and out of its utter emptiness, truly transformational truths can be heard—but only if we are still and quiet and linger to listen.

The Tao of George

There's a reason why *It's a Wonderful Life* is such an enduring film—and it's probably not what you think.

It's not just that certain copyright and licensing issues led to it airing every night on every station every holiday season for many years, making it as much a part of Christmas as trimming the tree and exchanging gifts.

It's not just that it's sweet or sentimental or so called Capracorn.

It's not just that it's an exceptionally written, perfectly acted and directed, inspiring and entertaining movie.

It's the Taoist-like balance it achieves, the yin-yang of its light and darkness, the truth of human existence it captures and conveys.

Birthed out of failure, *It's a Wonderful Life* began as a short story titled "The Greatest Gift," written by Philip Van Doren Stern, who, after failing to find a publisher for it, made it into a Christmas card, which he mailed to two hundred family members and friends. Originally purchased by RKO Pictures as a vehicle for Cary Grant, three different scripts were written and rejected before the project was shelved and Grant went on to make *The Bishop's Wife*—all of which led to Frank Capra getting involved and the success the film ultimately became. Of course, success is relative. This seminal, among-the-best-of-all-time movie was a box-office failure when first released in 1946.

George Bailey is a small-town man whose life seems so desperate he contemplates suicide. He had always wanted to leave Bedford Falls to see the world, but circumstances and his own good heart have led him to stay. He sacrificed his education for his brother's, kept the family-run savings and loan afloat, protected the town from the avarice of the greedy banker Mr. Potter, and married his childhood sweetheart. As he prepares to jump from a bridge, Clarence, his guardian angel, intercedes; showing him what life would have become for the residents of Bedford Falls if he had never lived—a hellish existence in the greed-driven, dark, depraved Pottersville.

Clarence tells George, "See, you've really had a wonderful life."

But has he?

As "wonderful" as George's life is—particularly in its positive impact on others, it's not all wonderful—or even good. There's a price to pay for living in a small town—or any size place where you don't fit in. There's a price to pay for honesty and integrity, for a life lived in service to others and high ideals—a high price for not having a price. The biggest price George pays is an internal one, intellectual and spiritual, the anguish and frustration that comes from being awake, surrounded by those who slumber.

Appropriately black and white, *It's a Wonderful Life* is profoundly Taoist in its push-pull of yin and yang. These two forces, and the interplay between them, arise out of emptiness—symbolized by the empty circle they are drawn into. George embodies, is surrounded by, and is acutely aware of light and dark, soft and hard, masculine and feminine, receptive and aggressive, but mostly the empty that is around and in and between all things. And it's this balance of the lighter and darker sides of existence that elevate this film to greatness. Without the one, you'd have silly, sweet, sentimental swill. Without the other, you'd have only meaninglessness and darkness. But the two together achieve a complexity and profundity that so mirrors reality it gives rise to the notion that life can actually imitate art.

Many viewers seem to miss how truly dark the film actually is, but it's this ingredient, this rich yinish quality that enables *It's a Wonderful Life* to earn its inspiration and ending.

The film's shadow side doesn't just appear when Bedford Falls transforms into Pottersville. It's been there all along—showing through the skein between realities, in the injustice and inequity, in the claustrophobia and frustration, in the way the rich and powerful oppress the poor and disenfranchised.

Perhaps more than an alternate reality, Pottersville is the same reality as Bedford Falls—only seen differently. George Bailey, a truly good, kind, and decent person, projects a goodness and decency on the world he inhabits. To him, the town is Bedford Falls. Old Man Potter has always seen it as Pottersville. The rich and powerful always view the world as theirs—their right, their entitlement, their prize, their reward. Instead of Pottersville being the version of reality that resulted from George never being born, maybe it's what happens when a good man like George finally allows the selfishness and brutishness and meaner aspects of lesser men to cloud his vision, when he gives up and gives in, quits fighting the good fight and turns the whole thing over to them.

The Tao is the way or path (a term used in a lot of the world's great wisdom traditions). It is ancient. Ineffable. Unnamable ("the Tao that can be named is not the Tao"). And you don't have to be Taoist to appreciate its universals truths or the wisdom of its most sacred text, the Tao Te Ching.

This way or channel is the flow of the universe. True fulfillment and serenity comes from living in harmony with it, walking the path. Like us, George spends much of his life fighting the path, stubbornly resisting the way, insisting he has a better way. Invariably, when he surrenders and begins to travel the way he glimpses his best self and begins to practice *wei wu wei*—doing without doing, actionless action, that in-the-zone alignment with the Tao, where we, like water, flow in a stream of effortless action/inaction, yielding, becoming inseparable, indistinguishable from the creator and all of creation. Truly one.

But George went to some very dark places before aligning himself with the Tao, before giving in and becoming truly free.

Like religion and philosophy, we turn to art for meaning—and few films are as meaningful and as much about meaning as *It's a Wonderful Life*. That an average George can make a difference, can have meaning by giving meaning to others, gives us hope, challenges us to make a difference. Viewing the film is a religious experience for me. Profound. Transcendent. Transformational. Watching it each year is a rite, a ritual, a memorial, and remembrance.

For me, *It's a Wonderful Life* is both inspirational and cathartic. It moves me like no other movie. I laugh and cry (a lot). I am George Bailey. I am small town. I have a small life. My Bedford Falls existence could easily be Pottersville if not for love, for art, for meaning, for family and friends. I'm on a quest, searching for meaning, attempting to walk the way. I want to make a difference in the world and doubt that I am doing much of anything that matters to much of anybody. George inspires me to give, to take the small gifts I've been given, like a few measly loaves and fish, and share them with others. It's what Philip Van Doren Stern did with his story, "The Greatest Gift." It's what I'm attempting to do at this very moment as I write this, for I believe what is written beneath the picture of George's dad in his office: "All you can take with you is that which you've given away."

Last Chance Romance

When we're young, possibilities seem endless, chances infinite. As we get older, as we journey further and further down the paths chosen, as we get further and further away from the paths not chosen, we realize how every choice is actually many choices—and how way leads on to way and we'll never be back to these particular two roads diverging in a yellow wood ever again. Every path we choose is also a choice against other paths, making our choices far more limited than we can even imagine, and as we continue on we see, tragically, how fewer and fewer choices we have left.

Most romance movies are, unfortunately, about young, pretty people, untouched by disappointment, unlined by time, who will live forever and who have an eternity of chances to squander, but occasionally a film comes along for grownups—one in which the potential lovers are a bit bent over and world-weary, aware, perhaps acutely, that soon one of the chances encountered will be their last.

This truth, this humbling awareness inspires sobriety and clarity, thoughtfulness and carefulness. These lovers aren't reckless with their chances for they know their chances aren't infinite. Perhaps this knowledge leads to a slight desperation, but more than anything it imbues them with a hesitancy I find irresistibly charming and gives them a gratitude for chances their younger selves took for granted.

Life has a way of lowering expectations (if our childhoods are good enough to make them high to begin with) and shattering illusions. What remains is far more real, far more interesting. It's part of why, even as time goes by, Rick and Ilsa of *Casablanca* are quintessential, timeless lovers. Though no Rick and Ilsa, Harvey Shine and Kate Walker are characters cut from the same well-worn cloth—elevated by the performances of well-worn actors Dustin Hoffman and Emma Thompson. Set in London, *Last Chance Harvey* is a romantic dramedy starring Hoffman as Harvey Shine, a divorced and haggard jingle-writer quickly aging out of his career and workaholic ways. With a warning from his boss (Richard Schiff) not to bother rushing back, Harvey goes to London, begrudgingly, for his daughter's wedding, desperately fielding work calls the whole time he's there.

When Harvey greets his estranged daughter, Susie (Liane Balaban), it becomes clear just how far away he's grown from his family. The film never spells out in exactly what ways Harvey was a bad father, but that Susie asks her stepfather (James Brolin) to give her away says it all. As Harvey leaves his heartbreak at the ceremony for an emergency work call, he misses his flight and gets fired.

Nursing a whiskey at the airport bar, Harvey bumps into Kate (Thompson), an airport employee escaping her own bad day with a glass of wine and a book. Suddenly taken by Kate's British charm, a tipsy Harvey bombards her with tales of his trouble. This unlikely trading of sob stories leads to lunch, a walk around London, and a day of unexpected romance.

Thompson and Hoffman bring far more to these characters than younger actors could (remind me again why our culture in general and Hollywood in particular is so obsessed with teens?), giving Kate and Harvey wit and charm just above their disappointments and essential sadness. *Last Chance Harvey* is slow paced (like its protagonists) and obvious in ways that border on cliché (and perhaps even crosses those borders sometimes), but it's also adultly romantic and sweet and sad.

Over a decade ago, while in my twenties, a woman told me I had the priorities of a much older man. It was one of the best compliments I received at the time, the only one I even remember, and sitting alone in the theater watching Harvey on the enormous screen, I thought the greatest thing I could take from his experience is not to wait until late in life to figure out what really matters. For even as a still sort of youngish man, it's possible that some seemingly random chance to be and act loving just might be my last.

Film Criticism

I'm not an expert on film (or anything else), but I *am* a student of it, and I've dabbled in it enough to know just how difficult it is to do well. I've taken a few film classes, I've written and sold screenplays, I've made a half-dozen short films and one handheld, no-budget feature, I've read hundreds of books on film and watched thousands of movies—just enough to know how very little I know.

Of course, you don't have to be an expert in or even a student of film to know just how challenging it is to make good ones—even the most casual moviegoer can tell you that more mediocre movies are made than anything else, and far, far more bad films are made than great ones.

Still, I find it a bit uncomfortable to criticize the state of American cinema. Part of the reason is in the difference in knowing and doing. I know a little about film, but I'm not a working filmmaker—and there's an enormous difference between the two. I feel far more comfortable speaking about the state of American publishing or criticizing novels because I'm a working novelist. But, here again, because I do it, because I know how difficult it is to do well, I find it difficult to be vitriolic or violent in the way so many haters online and in print are.

I recall a challenge John Mellencamp issued to haters years ago. "You make your best rock record and I'll make mine," he said, "and then we'll compare the two."

The point is well taken. Criticizing is easy. Creating enduring art isn't. And making an attempt at making authentic art gives us greater appreciation for all who do—regardless of the relative failure that results.

And it will fail. Everything does—particularly art. I understand this all too well. As Joyce Carol Oats observed, "The artist, perhaps more than any other person, inhabits failure."

This same sentiment is echoed in a remark by T.S. Eliot. When someone commented to him that most critics are failed writers, he responded, "So are most writers." I would say all. It's just some books fail less than others.

My approach to this book has been to reflect on life and meaning as I'm inspired by exemplary works of art, and with few exceptions—a few books and movies so bad I had to comment or mediocre works that nonetheless provoked thoughts I felt worth sharing—I've done just that, which casts me in the role of appreciater far more than criticizer.

But the state of Hollywood movies in general, and summer movies in particular, is so bad, I'm compelled to write about it, so, having said all the above, I will now step out of my role as appreciator and into the ill-fitting clothes of criticizer.

What's wrong with Hollywood?

It all comes down to character and story. We come to movies wanting an experience of what it means to be human. Whether in ordinary or extraordinary circumstances, we hunger for humanity— everything else is secondary. Everything—visuals, stunts, explosions, chases, spectacles. What's missing is humanity—people we can relate to in credible (if extraordinary or even unrealistic) situations.

And here's why: money.

Art for profit becomes entertainment. Entertainment produced to make the most money possible becomes hollow, shallow, silly, bloodless, lifeless.

Like politics and our "free" market, greed has largely spoiled the entertainment industry. Blockbuster-driven studios produce absurdly big-budget movies that, like other entities in our society are "too big to fail," and so try to be all things to all people, attempting an even more watered-down version of what worked before.

Sure, there are still a few auteurs around working within the studios, but most are forced to make independent films—something becoming increasingly difficult to do, with fewer and fewer means of distribution.

In the same way chain stores and blockbuster and celebrity books have negatively impacted publishing, Cineplexes, blockbuster movies, and star vehicles have hurt the film industry.

Here's my top-ten list of What's Wrong with Hollywood:

—Illiteracy. Too many people at the top making the biggest decisions don't read—not books and not even the scripts they're greenlighting.
—Gatekeepers. Interns are doing most of the reading, writing coverage, and, therefore, deciding.
—Risk aversion. Art can't be made without risk.
—Money. See above. Things are out of balance. Too much business, not enough show.
—Sequels. Enough!
—Old TV shows. Even if something happened to work as a television show, chances are it won't as a film. TV and film are different mediums—and it has little to do with the relative size of the screen.
—Video games. Really? Really?
—Pyrotechnics over people. If we don't care about your characters, we'll soon be bored with your explosions.
—Skewing tween. By attempting to make PG-13 movies for adults that appeal to tweens too, you do neither.
—3D. Gimmicks can't distract us from seeing that you have only cardboard characters and a preposterous plot—and having to see that in 3D just makes our heads ache all the more.

Wide Open Spaces
and the Sound of Silence

Quiet.

Slow-paced.

Character study.

Not words you'll hear used to market many movies—especially in the era of blockbusters and Cineplexes—but for a film to truly be affecting, to give us, its audience, the opportunity to connect with its characters, it must involve no small amount of moments that involve just such things.

In the same way each of us need time, silence, and solitude to become our best, deepest, richest, most inwardly complex selves, a film needs a certain pace and space for characters to live and breathe. A life fitted with time to think, space to meditate, to contemplate, to be, is essential for soul building. A story imbued with quiet not only allows character to develop, but enables us to connect.

And nothing's more important.

Stories are magic, are sacred things, because they give us multiple lives, infinite incarnations, endless opportunities to so identify with a character that we become that character, that we experience existence from inside another.

Of course, this can be done during the quiet moments between action sequences or battle scenes, but the more the moments, the more deeply we experience the other, and if an entire story is thus, well then, all the mo' betta'.

Crazy Heart is just such a story—a quiet, slow-paced, character study. Affecting. Moving. More.

Fifty-seven-year-old Bad Blake is a minor legend as a country singer. But that status only nets him gigs in bowling alleys and bars. Bad is an overweight, chain-smoking alcoholic. He is informed by a doctor that his self-destructive lifestyle will send him to an early grave. This self-destructive behavior has also led to several failed marriages and a grown son who he has not seen since he was four. While performing in Santa Fe, Bad meets newspaper journalist Jean Craddock, who wants to do a piece on him for her newspaper. Despite the differences in their ages, Jean and Bad begin a relationship. Jean and her four-year-old son Buddy become the closest thing to family Bad has. Not coincidentally, during this time he experiences a resurrection of sorts in his career, but what looks to be a promising professional and personal future may be jeopardized by his hell-bent self-destructiveness.

Crazy Heart is a good enough film, but it's the performances that elevate it into something worth recommending. Jeff Bridges and Maggie Gyllenhaal are quietly mesmerizing.

As I watched *Crazy Heart*, I kept thinking that what I was seeing was a remake—or at least the spiritual offspring—of *Tender Mercies*. And then Robert Duvall made an appearance (and later I found out he produced it), and it confirmed the connection between the two films for me.

Tender Mercies stars Robert Duvall (in an Oscar-winning performance) in a touching story of a down-and-out country singer named Mac Sledge who meets Rosa Lee, a young widow (Tess Harper) in a small Texas town. But as their relationship blossoms, Mac's years of hard living resurface when his music star ex-wife (Betty Buckley) appears, bringing his estranged daughter (Ellen Barkin) with her. It's a low-key, contemplative film directed by Australian Bruce Beresford (*Driving Miss Daisy*, *Breaker Morant*), written by Horton Foote (*To Kill a Mockingbird*), who won an Oscar for his screenplay.

Tender Mercies is that rare film that is far, far greater than the sum of its parts—a simple story told simply, its understated performances pitch-perfect for this masterpiece of quietude.

Both *Crazy Heart* and *Tender Mercies* are redemption stories set in the sad, alcohol-soaked world of country music, where the music itself is a character. Bad sings (and lives) that "falling feels like flying for a little while," and Mac keeps reminding himself over and over that no matter how painful, he must "face reality."

Though film as a medium is limited in showing it, simplicity in one's outer life often leads to richness and complexity in one's inner life. It's what Walden is about—going to the woods to live deliberately, to front only the essential facts of life, to learn what it has to teach, and not, when we die, discover that we had not lived.

It's a big part of why I live where I do (on a lake in a small town) and an even bigger part of why I live the *way* I do. Without time to think, without space to breathe, without stillness and solitude, we're like plants in a windowless, smoke-filled office, dying without sun and rain and fresh air. Whether we're confronting alcoholism or existentialism, we, like Bad Brad and Mac, need time and space and love.

Love changes us. It's the only thing that can. Actually, it's far more accurate to say that love gives us the opportunity, the environment, in which change can occur. Jean's love for Bad Blake, Rosa Lee's love for Mac Sledge, provide a milieu for the men to change—any substantive change they do.

Unconditional love is the greatest gift we can give ourselves and others.

Acceptance.

Being accepted—completely and utterly accepted—just as we are. No judgment. No rejection. No expectations. Nothing but passionate compassion, understanding, appreciation, kindness.

Rosa Lee's love for Mac is unconditional. She is constant. She is patient. She is giving. Mac experiences God's tender mercies through her—which is what makes this small, quiet film profound. She gives Mac something Jean isn't quite able to give Bad. The capacity for love each woman has is different. They are different and have had very different experiences.

Life is suffering—much of it unnecessary and self-inflicted—but, as Mac discovers, being loved, truly loved, makes even tragedy and trauma bearable. Trusting in, resting in, being secure in another's (and ultimately God's) love enables us not to survive life, but to experience it with hope and joy.

Mac tells Rosa Lee, "I don't trust happiness. I never have and

I never will," but despite his claim, and the way his self-destructive decisions have so often caused it to be true, her unconditional love is showing him day by day, moment by moment, he can trust goodness and good things.

And it's not just washed up, alcoholic country singers who need unconditional love. We all do. Unfortunately, too often when fronted with it, we find it so foreign, so inconceivable, we run from it. Mac jumps in the old pickup truck, buys a bottle, and runs as fast as he can, but something, thankfully, mercifully, brings him back.

What was it that brought him back? The kind, loving, and oh so tender mercies of a good woman (and God loving him through her).

Mix Tape Teen Romance

The music we listen to becomes the soundtracks of our lives. This is true nowhere more so than in adolescence—when music doesn't just move from background to foreground, but becomes the language we speak. Because of this, there is nothing quite like the poetry of the teenage romance mix tape—or its modern equivalent, the playlist.

Music is magical, and its enchanted ability to capture the emotions we can't express as teens, when we've yet to develop an adequate language for all we feel, is part of the magic of *Nick and Norah's Infinite Playlist*.

A boy and a girl. A night and a city. An infinite playlist. An infinite date. *Nick and Norah's Infinite Playlist* is a nocturnal indie rock odyssey romance that keeps it real.

Before *Nick and Norah's Infinite Playlist* was a hit movie, it was a hip, heady young-adult novel about two teens thrust together for one fun, funny, chaotic, sleepless night in a world of queer-core bands, teen hook-ups, and loud, live music.

Written in alternating his and her chapters by Rachel Cohn and David Levithan, the authors imbue their characters with passion, intelligence, and integrity, and treat their young audience with a rare respect, absent of any condescension. Cohn and Levithan demonstrate an impressively intimate knowledge of both contemporary teens and the

Manhattan indie rock scene. Both Nick and Norah are believable, fully
fleshed-out members of the YouTube, My Space, Facebook generation.
Perhaps the only two straight-edges out on this wild night, neither Nick
nor Norah drink or drug. Music, friends, and soon each other, not
mood-altering substances, are their obsessions.

The movie is good. The book is far better. But both novel and
film have scenes that give them depth and meaning, and elevate them
far beyond the typical teen romance into something like art—very much
like.

Of the many particularly poignant moments in a night full of
insight and revelation, here are my two favorites:

"There's one part of Judaism I really like," Norah says.
"Conceptually, I mean. It's called *tikkun olam*. Basically it
says that the world has been broken into pieces. All this
chaos, all this discord. And our job—everyone's job—is
to try to put the pieces back together. To make things
whole again."
Nick says, "Maybe we're the pieces. Maybe it isn't that
we're supposed to find the pieces and put them back
together. Maybe *we're* the pieces."
Or this scene when Nick is talking to his gay friend and
band member, Dev:
Dev glides his hand into mine and intertwines our
fingers.
"Other bands, it's about sex. Or pain. Or some fantasy.
But the Beatles, they knew what they were doing. You
know the reason the Beatles made it so big?"
"What?"
"'I wanna hold your hand.' First single. That's what
everyone wants. Not 24-7 hot wet sex. Not a marriage
that lasts a hundred years. They wanna hold your hand.
Every successful love story has those unbearable and
unbearably exciting moments of hand-holding."

I wanna hold Nick and Norah's hand. I wanna listen to their
infinite playlist over and over again. It holds not a single superfluous
song. They're the perfect tunes to connect to—to hold hands to, to
touch souls to, to fall in love to. And that's exactly what I did.

String Theory

I'm always interested in the emergence of similar themes in movies—not trends that have an innovator and imitators, but films released so closely together it seems their creators were having the same dream.

Two recent films exploring the same issue (namely, is it possible for a man and a woman to have a purely sexual relationship?) are *Love and Other Drugs* and *No Strings Attached*. And though both approach the subject in different ways, with different characters and setups, they have enough in common to inspire a look at their underlying cultural significance. My guess is that for these two films that actually got the green light, hundreds of scripts representing variations on this same theme were tossed over many an agent's transom.

So, why all this interest in sex-only scenarios? Why is "friends with benefits" so popular? The primary reasons given for the purely sexual relationships in the movies are to avoid pain and complications. Is this a result of a generation reacting to their parents' bad breakups? A defensive stance against the cost of caring and the inevitability of heartache? Is it the result of feminism? Porn? The masculinization of relationships? The moving onto the mainstream radar of alternate ways of being and relating? I'd say it's some of all the above.

Regardless of the relationship configuration—friends, lovers, partners, sex buddies, or any combination or variation—the two things that are unavoidable are the very things the couples in each movie are attempting to avoid. When we invite someone into our lives—in any capacity at all—we are inviting pain and complications. This is particularly true of friends and lovers.

The Buddha said life is suffering.

It's part of life. It *is* life.

Jesus said compassion—the act of feeling what others feel, including their pain—is the most like God we can be.

To me, the relevant question is not "Is it possible to have a relationship that avoids suffering and complications?" but "Why would you want one?" Life is messy. We are the children of the big, green, slimy mama. We are complex beings fashioned in the likeness of God, the contradiction, according to the biblical book of Genesis, of lofty spirit and lowly dirt, animal and spiritual. Can we really join ourselves with other such creatures without über complications, heartache, friction, frustration, pain, joy, ecstasy, creativity, love, anger, challenge, difficulty, meaning, and madness? And if we could, why would we want to?

Nietzsche said, "There is always some madness in love. But there is also always some reason in madness," and Francoise Sagan said, "I have loved to the point of madness, That which is called madness, That which to me, Is the only sensible way to love." To me, both quotes resonate within this anonymous one: "A fool in love makes no sense to me. I only think you are a fool if you do not love."

The gentle madness of love that makes fools of us all is not to be avoided, but sought. The fact that, as Shakespeare so insightfully noted, "the course of true love never did run smooth," is the whole point.

Of course, it's human nature, or seems to be, to avoid suffering, to search for the situation that gives the most pleasure for the least personal cost. And that's exactly what the characters of these two films attempt.

In *No Strings Attached*, Emma (Natalie Portman) and Adam (Ashton Kutcher) are life-long friends who almost ruin everything by having sex one morning. In order to protect their friendship, they make a pact to keep their relationship strictly "no strings attached." "No strings" means no jealousy, no expectations, no fighting, no flowers, no baby voices. It means they can do whatever they want, whenever they want, in whatever public place they want, as long as they don't fall in love. The questions become: Can you have sex without love getting in the way? And can their friendship survive?

In *Love and Other Drugs*, Maggie (Anne Hathaway) is an alluring free spirit who won't let anyone—or anything—tie her down. But she meets her match in Jamie (Jake Gyllenhaal), whose relentless and nearly infallible charm serves him well with the ladies and in the cutthroat world of pharmaceutical sales. Maggie and Jamie's evolving relationship takes them both by surprise, as they find themselves under the influence of the ultimate drug—love.

Neither picture is great, and though *Love and Other Drugs* is the better film, both are entertaining, have moments of humor and insight, and really strong performances from their respective stars and supporting cast. As usual, Natalie Portman stands out—something she's been doing since *Leon: The Professional* and all the way through *Beautiful Girls, Garden State, V for Vendetta, Closer*, and again just recently in *Black Swan*.

But far more interesting than any performance or even the films themselves is the lengths we go to in order to avoid pain and heartache and complication and vulnerability and, yes, madness. We're defending against the things we need most—loss of control, ego death, connection, compassion, need, want, desire, love.

Our souls need the complexity and difficulty and challenge and pain of relationships. We cannot become who we're meant to be without them. The notion that we can have lovers with no strings or sex with no complications is a denial of the soul and assumes choosing who we love and get involved with is somehow a rational decision up to us, but as Rumi said, "Lovers don't finally meet somewhere. They're in each other all along." Our souls find each other, are drawn together by forces we can scarcely imagine, and our connections accomplish things within us we can't begin to comprehend—and it doesn't get much more complicated or stringy than that.

Changeling—a True, True Story

There are movies. There are films. Then, there is art.

Zack and Mira Make a Porno is a movie. *Appaloosa* is a film. Clint Eastwood's *Changeling* is a work of art.

Changeling is a quiet masterpiece by a seventy-eight-year-old auteur who has at least three things in common with my favorite director Alfred Hitchcock. Both Eastwood and Hitchcock did their best work late in life (after a lifetime of good work). Both filmmakers functioned as independents within the studio system. And both enjoy commercial and critical success.

Of course, Eastwood isn't the only artist involved in *Changeling*. Screenwriter Michael Straczynski turns in a stellar novel-like script and Angelina Jolie is beyond brilliant in an understated and deeply affecting performance.

Set in 1928 Los Angeles, *Changeling* is the story of a single mother, Christine Collins, who returns home one day to discover her nine-year-old son, Walter, missing. Several months later, Christine is told that her son has been found alive, but when Christine sees Walter she doesn't recognize him. Captain Jones pressures a confused Christine into taking the boy home "on a trial basis."

After Christine confronts Captain Jones with physical discrepancies between the little boy claiming to be Walter and her son, Jones orders Christine to the Los Angeles County Hospital's psychopathic ward, and she is told repeatedly that if she will just admit she was mistaken about Walter and say the LAPD was right, she'll be released.

What really happened to Walter Collins is later revealed. Sort of. But this powerful story is not so much about the abduction or the investigation, but the faith and fortitude of a powerless single mother in the face of the all-powerful, male-dominated, corrupt police department. It's a reminder of how easily power is abused, and how very much accountability and checks and balances are essential to protect citizens from their government.

Heroic people abound in this story. There's Christine Collins, of course, but there's also the outspoken minister, Gustav Briegleb, and Detective Ybarra (Michael Kelly) who conducts the actual investigation into what happened to Walter Collins in spite of enormous pressure by Captain Jones not to do so. And, as usual, heroes are ordinary people just being decent human beings when the entire mighty rushing river of corrupt culture is pounding them, pushing them to conform, to go along to get along, to let go and just go with the flow.

The highest compliment I can give the near-perfect, perhaps even perfect, *Changeling* is that it is a true story. And I don't just mean that is was based on real people and actual events, but that it is true in every single sense of the word. If fiction is the lie that tells the truth, then this story is the truth that tells an even deeper truth. *Changeling* is a deeply, devastatingly, powerfully, profoundly true work of art, and it doesn't get any truer than that.

We'll Always Have *Casablanca*

Finding a good film to experience seems an increasingly impossible proposition, but each time a new one fails to live up to its promise, I remind myself that we in the cinephile community will always have *Casablanca*.

Not only is *Casablanca* the best, most beloved, most enduring film in cinematic history, it happens to be one of my favorites. I discovered it while in college, and have watched it countless times since then—probably pushing thirty times by now. It moves me to a depth that only films like *It's a Wonderful Life* and *Keys of the Kingdom* and a very few others can.

Casablanca is a unique story of a love triangle set against the high stakes of World War II. Humphrey Bogart plays the allegedly apolitical club owner in unoccupied French territory that is nevertheless crawling with Nazis; Ingrid Bergman is the lover who mysteriously deserted him in Paris; and Paul Heinreid is her heroic, slightly bewildered husband. Claude Rains, Sydney Greenstreet, Peter Lorre, and Conrad Veidt are among what is undoubtedly the best supporting cast in history.

Casablanca is many things—adventure/suspense/intrigue/wartime story, a dramatic, comedic, ultimately tragic true tale; but more than anything else, it's a romance. *Casablanca* has style and substance. It's inspiring and thought-provoking and highly entertaining, but beneath it all, amidst it all, suffusing every frame is a rare, wildly romantic, once-in-a-lifetime love that lasts and lasts as time goes by.

Casablanca is pure magic, a mystery, a miracle of the old Hollywood studio system. It was one of fifty films made by Warner Brothers in 1942—just another picture produced in the film factory that turned out features the way production companies do television shows today—only more of them. The actors, all under contract, had just finished making other movies, and would each start others soon after this one wrapped. The director had already directed over forty films. The writer (after the amazing Epstein brothers were pulled off for another project) was merely a junior member of the Warner's writing pool. The script was based on an unproduced play that James Agee called one of the world's worst. War effort movies were a dime a dozen. All this and yet a masterpiece was made—not just another picture, but the greatest film of all time.

Sometimes magic happens. Everything comes together in ways that are unpredictable, unexpected, unimaginable. When this happens, we're reminded that there are forces greater than ourselves involved, and that sometimes, just sometimes, we are part of something transcendent—that what is created, in this case *Casablanca*, is far greater than the sum of its parts.

What makes *Casablanca* the greatest film of all time?

There are so many things. The theme of sacrifice and redemption—*Casablanca* is a uniquely hard-boiled romance. The chemistry between Bogart and Bergman. The stellar cast—every single role is filled by a gifted actor, perfectly cast. The setting—exotic, yet accessible, foreign, yet familiar; the film drips with atmosphere. The music. The set design. The wardrobe.

A better question is what doesn't contribute to making it the greatest film ever made? The only things I can think of—logic issues with the story or the shortcomings in the rear-projection work, or the lack of directorial style—are technicalities, and not even noticeable because of the way every other element forces us to willingly, gladly, inevitably suspend disbelief.

All these factors contribute to the film's greatness, but the single most important element is its script.

There's a reason for the old Hollywood adage, "It's possible to make a bad movie out of a good script, but impossible to make a good movie out of a bad script." Not only is the script the most fundamental, foundational element of a film, but it's the single most import.

The writing in *Casablanca* is stellar—entertaining, elegant, urbane, sophisticated, funny, insightful, and witty. Even among the star-filled galaxy of the greatest scripts ever written, *Casablanca* shines brightest, providing some of the most memorable moments in movie history, some of the most oft-quoted lines—all because of how deftly it combines cleverness, wit, drama, adventure, comedy, insight, characterization, realism, idealism, romanticism, and cynicism, while entertaining audiences with every single word.

Not only has *Casablanca* given us cultural catchphrases like "We'll always have Paris," "Here's looking at you, Kid," etc., but it has also given us some of the most well-written scenes in the history of motion pictures—scenes so complex, so suffused with subtext and nuance they can be watched over and over, revealing new insights with each subsequent viewing. In his enormously popular principles of screenwriting book, *Story*, Robert McKee uses *Casablanca* over and over as an example of successful screenwriting. So great is my admiration and appreciation for the writing, I have included lines from and scenes inspired by *Casablanca* in several of my novels and stories, including *Blood of the Lamb*, *Thunder Beach*, and "Death at the Crossroads" in the anthology *Delta Blues*.

Here are a couple of examples of the humor, wit, and intelligence in the script:

Major Strasser: What is your nationality?
Rick: I'm a drunkard.
Captain Renault: That makes Rick a citizen of the world.

Captain Renault: What in heaven's name brought you to Casablanca?
Rick: My health. I came to Casablanca for the waters.
Captain Renault: The waters? What waters? We're in the desert.
Rick: I was misinformed.

Captain Renault: Carl, see that Major Strasser gets a good table, one close to the ladies.
Carl: I have already given him the best, knowing he is German and would take it anyway.

Part of the reason the film endures is because of its timeless quality. And it's not just that its characters and themes and situations are timeless, but its photography. Had *Casablanca* been a color picture, it would be locked into the technological limitations of its time, but its glorious black-and-white images are even more luminous today than they were in 1942, making *Casablanca* an ethereal, eternal place we can visit regardless of the time and space we're bound by.

Casablanca is a moral movie, a propaganda piece that never feels like anything but sheer entertainment. It endures because it's about good people, committed to the greater good, to the cause of freedom and justice—so much so that they will sacrifice their great, once-in-a-lifetime love, even their own lives. Rick and Ilsa are heroes, for they love the fight for right even more than that which they most want in the wide world—to be with each other.

In the end, a cynic becomes a romantic, then an idealist, then a hero. Love changes Rick. Love changes everything. Rick and Ilsa get Paris back and in the process, Rick gets his soul back. Redemption has rarely been as profound, moving, or entertaining.

Arise My Love

The Adjustment Bureau, which has moments reminiscent of *The Matrix* and *Dark City*, is at heart a romance far more than sci-fi flick. In fact, its use of science fiction and fantasy elements only serve as obstacles for its lovers and as catalysts for philosophical explorations of fate and free will, ambition and amorousness.

As I sat in the theater watching the lovers fight for their fate, battle forces beyond them, passages from The Song kept echoing through my mind—as did *Eternal Sunshine of the Spotless Mind*, another film that brought to mind The Song.

The Song (or Song of Songs) is a book of Egyptian love poetry found in the heart of the Hebrew Bible. It's provocative and profound, sensual and sexual, powerfully capturing both the desires of lovers and the hostility of others to them and their love.

The world is hostile to love and lovers. It has been ever thus.

In The Song, the lover calls to her beloved, saying:

Arise, my love,
my fair one, and come away;
for now the winter is past, the rain is over and gone.
The flowers appear on the earth;
the time of singing has come.

Arise, my love, my fair one, and come away.
She has been searching the city for her lover and
experienced firsthand just how cruel the heartless
townsmen can be:
I run out after him, calling,
but he is gone.
The men who roam the streets,
guarding the walls,
beat me and tear away my robe.

The lovers only hope is to flee to the countryside, to find a garden so they can be alone—away from the callous, commerce-driven city, away from those who find love superfluous, frivolous, worthless.

Lovers retreat into one another—not only because each is the other's first, best sanctuary, but because there is often no other safe place.

As Rumi puts it:

Lovers find secret places
inside this violent world
where they make transactions
with beauty.

This is some of what I was thinking as David Norris chased Elise Sellas and agents of the adjustment bureau chased them both through the city.

On the brink of winning a seat in the U.S. Senate, ambitious politician David Norris (Matt Damon) meets beautiful contemporary ballet dancer Elise Sellas (Emily Blunt)—a woman like none he's ever known. But just as he realizes he's falling for her, mysterious men conspire to keep the two apart.

David learns he is up against the agents of fate itself—the men of the adjustment bureau—who will do everything in their considerable power to prevent David and Elise from being together. In the face of overwhelming odds, he must either let her go and accept a predetermined path—or risk everything to defy fate and be with her.

Lovers facing obstacles to be together may be the oldest plot in the history of story—or at least second behind adventure tales of the hunt around cave fires. But the obstacles—whether agents from the adjustment bureau or mundane things far less dramatic—aren't just conflict-producing plot points but examples of art imitating life. Most lovers know only too well just how difficult it is to make love stay.

And what of choosing a lover, choosing to love or not? Or any number of other decisions we make, or think we do, every day? Do we have free will? Are we truly free? In the world of the movie, we're not. Unseen forces influence and adjust. It's an interesting notion. Even a nonconformist iconoclast like me often questions how free I really am. And you don't have to believe in fate or full blown determinism to see how way leads to way, how every choice limits subsequent choices, how our paradigms and worldviews and cultures and educations and families and religions, like the agents of the adjustment bureau, exert enormous, often unseen influence on us.

One of the more intriguing questions raised by the film concerns coupling and accomplishment, happiness and ambition. Does being in a fulfilling relationship cause us to be less driven, to do less with our lives? Does love makes us lose our edge? Fill a crevice without which we fill with other often obsessive pursuits and passions? David is told that if he and Elise become each other's, neither will live up to their considerable potential, that to become her lover means forfeiting the White House and the opportunity to change the world.

This is something I've wondered about nearly as long as I can recall—am I limited as an artist by my happy childhood and love-filled life?

Perhaps a better question is, so what? So what if David and Elise do less in the world? So what if the mundane aspects of life together make them more mundane as people? I'm not convinced it does—or has to—but so what if it does? What of love? What of what it produces in our souls, the mark it leaves on us that is anything but mundane? Isn't that worth the White House and any number of accomplishments? And what if love is all there is? What if love and lover are all—everything and anything else a distraction, an illusion, a poor substitute?

Again, Rumi:

> Be foolishly in love
> for love is all there is.
> There is no way into presence

except through a love exchange.
Love and lover live in eternity.
Other desires are substitutes
for that way of being.

My Not So Guilty Pleasure

The film editor of *Crime Spree Magazine*, Jeremy Lynch, asked me
to contribute an essay to a series he's running about guilty pleasures.

After I agreed to do it and began to think about it, I realized I
don't really have any. Guilt, like shame and fear and envy and hate, is a
negative, mostly useless emotion. I experience remorse when I realize
I've been wrong (which is often) and do my best to take responsibility
for it, repent, and attempt to rectify the situation. But I associate guilt
with feelings produced by cultural and parental programming, voices
of shame inside us that don't lead to change, but only to continual
condemnation.

I'm in no way saying I never feel guilt. I do—even the negative,
waste-of-time kind. But I do my best to identify it and eighty-six it as
quickly as possible.

I live a very deliberate life—one, as much as possible, from my
soul, by my design, based on my callings and convictions, not those
of the culture around me. In this, I feel a deep kinship to Emerson,
attempting to be and not conform, to, as he said, "Be, and not seem."

Given this, and my conviction that, as Emerson said, "genuine
action will explain itself," I try neither to do anything because of how
it looks or apologize for anything I do—and this includes movies. But
when thinking of guilty pleasures, two genres come to mind—romance

and horror.

I don't feel guilty about the films I enjoy in either genre because I'm very selective, but both genres seem to have an inordinate amount of inanity and insipidity, movies deserving of the "guilty pleasure" moniker.

For my not-so-guilty "guilty pleasure," I choose a horror movie.

Recently, I drove over and took my soon-to-be twenty-one-year-old daughter to the midnight showing of *Scream 4*.

And you're thinking, surely I should feel guilty about that, right? Well, I don't. Not even a little. And here's why: not only is *Scream 4* a smart, funny, self-conscious, suspenseful meta-art masterpiece, but well-made suspense-based horror movies are something I've used to connect with my daughter since her early adolescence when I had to tell her what parts to close her eyes during.

In the fourth *Scream* installment, Sidney Prescott, now the author of a self-help book, returns home to Woodsboro on the last stop of her book tour. Unfortunately, Sidney's appearance also brings about the return of Ghostface, putting Sidney, her old friends, Gale and Dewey, along with her teenage niece Jill and her friends, in danger.

I don't care for horrific or shocking images, don't like to be subjected to what has come to be known as the torture porn. But I do love suspense—the art of *Psycho*, the German Expressionism and relentless tension of the original *Halloween*, the Hitchcockian brand of anxiety that causes an audience to forget to breathe. And I appreciate smart, well-written scripts. *Scream 4* has a bit of both of these—along with humor and hipness to spare.

Like the original, and to a lesser extent the other two sequels, *Scream 4* works on a lot of levels, but is perhaps at its best when exploring genre. It not only looks at horror genre conventions in general, but at the micro sub-genre of *Scream* itself. At one point I thought, I'm sitting in a theater watching a movie in which kids inside a movie are watching a movie based on a movie based on a book based on a movie—and in the process the characters are not only talking about the other movies, but the one they're in.

If you like smart, hip, fun, suspenseful horror with all of the pleasure and none of the guilt, treat yourself to *Scream 4*.

Conversations with Women Before Sunrise

Few things in life are more meaningful than a meaningful conversation.

A dialog is an exchange not just of words and ideas, thoughts and feelings, but of our very selves. As we talk, closely, intimately, we actually breathe in each other.

Though I've enjoyed many great conversations with male friends, there's something about conversations with women that take talk to a whole other dimension. Women are typically more communicative, start at an earlier age (therefore, have had more practice), and are usually more willing to invest the time a great conversation usually requires.

I don't just enjoy conversations in life, but in art, as well.

Some of my favorite films, particularly romances, are little more than a guy and a girl having a conversation.

Of course, in a way, every love story is a conversation between two lovers, even classics like the Song of Songs and *Romeo and Juliet*, but the dialog often involves others—family, friends, even adversaries. And as good as these kinds of love stories can be, there's something special about the stripped-down, essential nature of two lovers having one long, uninterrupted conversation that I find more intense, intimate, inspiring.

I'm focusing here on the magic that's possible between a guy and a girl, but I in no way think it can only happen between a guy and a girl, or one guy and one girl. Two guys or two girls or three or five can be just as true, just as intense, just as revealing. For me, heterosexuality and monogamy are not requirements.

The two very best long-form conversations in film, the purest examples of the form, and the ones that have my highest recommendation are *Before Sunset* and *Conversations with Other Women*. These two extraordinary films take something quite ordinary—former lovers having a conversation—and elevate it to the realm of truth and art and pain and beauty and loss, and for a brief moment make us feel less alone in the world.

Before Sunset has the added advantage of an earlier film that shows the same two lovers in a long, uninterrupted conversation nearly a decade earlier in *Before Sunrise*. In fact, *Before Sunrise* is a great film in its own right, but I find far more depth and meaning in the older lovers and in their pain and loss and regret-tinged conversation than in that of the young, hopeful, mostly unscarred, a-little-too-removed-from-it-all, whole-life-in-front-of-them kids they were when they first met.

In both *Before Sunset* and *Conversations with Other Women*, pain and loss and disappointment suffuse the subtext and prevent the lovers from being too cool or cavalier about life or love or each other.

And in each film, the lovers converse under the looming deadline—the sun setting, a plane's departure—of a forced parting. Far more than a dramatic device, for me this represents how finite all our connections are, how short life itself is, how important it is to make each and every word of every conversation count.

The films remind us that we have a limited supply of words, sentences, encounters, connections. *Ultima forsan*, "perhaps the last"—something I have written into the flesh of my arm so as not to forget—every moment, every encounter, every sentence, every single word could be our last, and soon one, in the too-near future, will be.

House of Pain

Like most of the best things in my life, I came to *House* because of a woman. And not just any woman, but one of the most beautiful, smart, strong, sexy, attractive actresses on the planet.

I had been hearing great things about the new medical mystery drama *House* for a while, but had never watched it for two reasons—I watch very limited TV; and as a rule don't start a series midway through. Then I heard Sela Ward would be joining the cast for a multi-episode arc, and knew I would gladly add another show to my must-sees, and start in the middle or even the end if I had to. Thankfully, because of TV on DVD, I didn't have to.

Most people think of *Sisters* when Sela Ward's name comes up, but it was as Lily Manning on *Once and Again* that I fell in love with her, and, for me, she will always be the sexy, recently single mother, vulnerable Venus—smart, compassionate, resilient.

As Stacy Warner, Sela Ward was actually a romantic equal to Hugh Laurie's Greg House, but alas, nothing lasts. House destroys what he has—or could have had—with Stacy; Sela's arc ends, Stacy leaves the show.

But I keep watching.

Though I originally tuned in for Sela, I kept tuning in for *House*.

One of the best-written and bravest shows on network

television, *House* has, for over a hundred episodes now, been consistently good and often great. Each year, as I watch the season finale, I always think, they'll never be able to top it—and then they do. Year after year after year, they leave me truly grateful for the engaging, enriching, and highly entertaining experiences they give me.

I have a friend who says *House* is too formulaic, and she's right that the medical mysteries always follow the pattern of a series of misdiagnoses, failed treatments, and eventually House's "aha" moment, but watching *House* for the medicine is like reading Shakespeare for the plot.

I watch *House*, like all the shows I watch, the novels I read, the films I watch, for the characters—the struggles and drama of their lives, their interactions with one another.

From the fist moment I watched the show, I thought, Greg House is Sherlock Holmes with a medical degree—a true anti-social, drug-addicted, music-playing, genius operating at a level that leaves mere mortals breathless and bewildered.

Like a fully functioning adult trying to get extremely important tasks completed with a team of impaired children, House lives in a state of perpetual frustration—add to it the physical pain Holmes never had and you have one unpleasant SOB.

Physician heal thyself? I'm not sure he would if he could, but he can't. None of us can. We have our part to play in the healing process, sure (I'm not advocating passivity), but it's in letting love in, letting fear and unforgiveness go—things House is unwilling to do.

Like Holmes, House needs constant challenges for his magnificent mind—puzzles, conundrums, mysteries. So much so that he plays mind games with the lesser planets orbiting the enormous gravitational pull of his imploding star.

Unlike Holmes, who rarely interacted with anyone beyond Watson, House, who avoids patients as much as possible, is forced to work with a team, answer to an administrator, and interact with a friend, which is what makes the show work so well.

Like Paul Weston of *In Treatment*, House is a wounded healer, but unlike Weston, House, who's in constant pain—and not just from the nerve damage in his leg—inflicts a lot of pain on others. Even those he heals. And unlike Weston, House takes no joy in healing, just hungers for the next mystery to apply his mind to.

Like Irene Adler was to Holmes, Sela Ward's Stacy Warner will always be for House *the* woman. Now that she's come and gone and come and gone again, House, who never really had even the remotest chance for happiness, is a miserable, broken, mean misanthrope—the most interesting one in the history of TV.

Like House, we're all in pain. Maybe ours is more intermittent, more manageable, but it's there—even when we're too distracted to notice it very much. We have the existential pain of mortality if nothing else (though usually there's plenty else—including the pain of others our compassion makes us heir to). Even in those rare, perfect moments of our lives when all is right with the world and we are as perfectly happy as we can be, its edges are tinged with the certainty that it can't last, that the moment will too soon be gone—and so will we. But instead of popping Vicodin, we can watch House do it, share in his suffering, share some of our own. That's the power of story. Stories heal. That's why for viewers, the *House* of pain can also be a place of healing.

The World Forgetting,
by the World Forgot

Long before this year of revolution and reading and best-actress Oscar, Kate Winslet was Clementine Kruczynski in Charlie Kaufman's brilliant and altogether original *Eternal Sunshine of the Spotless Mind.*

Kaufman's work is always thought-provoking, inspiring, and mystical, but even in such stellar company, *Eternal Sunshine of the Spotless Mind* stands out as the brightest object in his creative constellation.

Because of its neo-surrealistic elements, non-linear narrative, and its depiction of the degrading memories of its main characters, the film can be challenging, but it's not inaccessible—and that it requires us to pay attention only adds to its power.

Joel is stunned to discover that his girlfriend Clementine has had her memories of their tumultuous relationship erased. Out of desperation, he contracts the same team to have Clementine removed from his own memory. But as Joel's memories progressively disappear, he rediscovers their earlier passion. From deep within the recesses of his brain, Joel attempts to escape the procedure. As the team chase him through the maze of his memories, it's clear that Joel just can't get Clementine out of his head.

This rich, textured film has many themes, but the persistence of love is chief among them. I say persistence, but perhaps a better word is relentlessness. Maybe this is why the movie resonates with me so much. I believe in love above all else, in its eternal nature, in its relentless pursuit of the beloved. For me, God is love and love is god.

But love isn't just relentless, it's also painful. Joel and Clementine get hurt and hurt each other.

Life involves suffering. Love involves pain.

What to do?

The Buddha teaches that she who loves ten has ten woes, he who loves twenty has twenty woes. Jesus, whose teachings mirror those of the Buddha in so many ways, says the same thing, but whereas the Buddha's solution is to detach and end desire, Jesus says to love all the more—hurt with and for others, open ourselves up to the pain that comes from loving others with the full awareness that this will happen. Be compassionate as God is compassionate—actually feeling what others feel.

Joel and Clementine go to the ultimate extreme to erase their painful memories of one another—one not available to those of us outside a world created by Kaufman, but we've certainly become an overly medicated, overly stimulated, overly busy, overly shallow people attempting to avoid or numb pain. Denial. Distraction. Intoxication. What's our drug of choice to anesthetize ourselves from the unwanted gifts life gives? How many of us would choose to erase painful memories if the technology existed?

Like too many lovers, Joel and Clementine too quickly take each other for granted, grow complacent, but their lack of passion is a personal failing, and not one of the relationship. Like so many, they "fell" in love with the romantic ideal they were projecting onto each other and expected far more from the other than the other has to give. And like so many couples, the very things that initially attract them to each other later became the very things that repel them.

But there's an essential sweetness to Joel and Clementine that fits so well with Alexander Pope's poem that provides the title for the film:

> How happy is the blameless vestal's lot! The world
> forgetting, by the world forgot. Eternal Sunshine of
> the Spotless Mind! Each pray'r accepted, and each wish
> resign'd.

For all their flaws, Joel and Clementine are guileless.

Memory is magical—something *Eternal Sunshine of the Spotless Mind* captures in dense and nuanced ways. And like the film, our memories are continually invading our present moments—informing, influencing, inspiriting.

Love, even our flawed, faulty, fragile love, is worth fighting for. Joel and Clementine realize this. I hope we will. As I watched the two lovers running away from the team trying to erase their memories of one another, I couldn't help but think about the Song of Songs from the Hebrew Bible, and how its lovers, too, had to flee the city and those hostile to their love into the countryside to be alone.

Arise, my love, my beautiful one, and come away,
for behold, the winter is past; the rain is over and gone.
The flowers appear on the earth, the time of singing has
come.
Arise, my love, and come.

Whether Joel and Clementine realize it, whether you and I realize it, it's not just our lovers calling to us, but love itself.

Love is relentless. Give in.

Love opens us to pain. Embrace and experience it.

Love is god. God is love. Accept it.

Fight for love as Joel and Clementine do. Move heaven and earth if you have to. What else is worth fighting for?

Walking in Another's Shoes Whether They Fit or Not

I wish we lived in a world of love—of justice and compassion— where there was no judgment, only acceptance and appreciation. If this is too much to ask for, I wish we lived in a world where people were not judged by the color of their skin or their sex or their religion or their sexual orientation, but by the content of their character. If this is too much to ask for, then I wish we lived in a world where ignorance and hatefulness and incivility were marginalized instead of celebrated, where people who practice such things were not promoted to the top of companies, voted into office, given radio and TV shows and book deals. If this, too, is too much to ask for, then I at least wish those of us who disdain such things would not remain quiet, not give in to the blusterous bullies and their benighted rhetoric, not sit in silence as the insecure haters make homophobic, sexist, or racists remarks, not stand idly by accepting injustice because that's just the way the world works. As Dr. King said, "In the end, we will remember not the words of our enemies, but the silence of our friends."

To all this, you may say that I'm a naïve dreamer. Perhaps. But I'm not the only one.

There's King and Lennon, of course. And there's also Philip

Green—a highly respected writer who is recruited by a national magazine to write a series of articles on anti-Semitism in 1940s America in Elia Kazan's *Gentleman's Agreement*. Green (played by Gregory Peck) is not too hip on the idea at first, but then it occurs to him that since he's new in town, he can pretend to be Jewish, and thus experience firsthand the realities of racism and prejudice, and write from that perspective. It takes very little time for him to experience bigotry. He soon learns the liberal-minded firm he works for doesn't hire Jews and that his own secretary changed her name and kept the fact that she is Jewish a secret from everyone. Green soon finds that he won't be invited to certain parties, that he cannot stay in certain "restricted" hotels, and that his own son is called names in the street. His anger at the way he is treated also affects his relationship with his fiancée, Kathy Lacy, his publisher's niece and the person who suggested the series in the first place.

Of all the horrible injustices and inequities Green experiences, the most insidious is the silence Dr. King talked about, the gentleman's agreement of those who say they are not anti-Semitic not to stand up against those who are. Of course, by their very refusal to take a stand, they (and we) are part of the systemic oppression of the minority, the different, the other, that history gives dreadful witness to.

Gentleman's Agreement deals with anti-Semitism, but the lessons of hate and tribalism in the film apply to all oppressed peoples and groups, particularly the powerless, the different, the disenfranchised minority.

Gentleman's Agreement is a brave and poignant film—especially for 1947—and though I'm sure some will condemn it as polemical or didactic, I think it achieves a good balance between story and moral, never becoming preachy or patronizing. And it's not bulky or heavy-handed in the way of 2004's *Crash*.

Of all the brilliant achievements of *Gentleman's Agreement*, perhaps the two most telling and terrifying are the way good, well-intentioned people contribute to the oppression of others by not raging against the machine, and the way certain people within oppressed groups attempt to assimilate and disappear, and resent those who don't—both groups taking a dangerous "don't ask, don't tell" approach that requires denial and dishonesty.

Bigotry, prejudice, hate—any form of xenophobia, whether racism, sexism, classism, or homophobia—all come from the same little lizard brain place of fear that leads to tribalism, insecurity, and a warped sense of superiority.

I returned to *Gentleman's Agreement* recently for what must be the fifth viewing because of an experience I had that was not unlike that of Philip Green.

When word got out that I refused to be married until my gay brothers and sisters enjoyed the same opportunities and equality, gossip began to spread and certain people assumed I was gay and began treating me differently. Speculation and gossip and condemnation have continued and led to some incivility and unkindness—and the entire experience made me feel like I was living my own little version of *Gentleman's Agreement.*

I'm grateful for the experience, and its heightening of my experience of the film, which is rich and rewarding, reminding us that all that is necessary for the triumph of evil is that good people do nothing.

Gentleman's Agreement is filled with good people—actors, writers, filmmakers—doing something.

Several of the main players and the director of *Gentleman's Agreement* were brought before the House Un-American Activities Committee. The two who refused to testify, John Garfield (who played Green's best friend, Dave Goldman) and Anne Revere (who played Green's mother) were added to the Hollywood Blacklist. Revere didn't appear in another movie for twenty years and Garfield died of a heart attack at the age of thirty-nine after being called before the committee again—this time to testify against his wife.

Gregory Peck, my all-time favorite actor, for his choice of roles even more than his acting style and screen presence, was a good, principled man whose name was on Richard Nixon's "enemies list." Peck *is* Philip Green, Father Chisholm, Dr. Anthony Edwards, Joe Bradley, King David, and Atticus Finch—the very embodiment of the best of the characters he played.

Our failures of compassion say far more about us than those we're prejudiced against. And compassion is the key—not pity that comes from a superior place, but a "feeling with," putting ourselves in the place of others, experiencing what they experience, feeling what they feel. As another of Gregory Peck's characters, Atticus Finch, says, "You never really understand a person until you consider things from his point of view—until you climb into his skin and walk around in it." A Muslim proverb says, "To understand a person, you must walk a mile in her shoes whether they fit or not." It's exactly what Atticus Finch and Philip Green do, and what you and I can do every day, if we will only be as willing and caring and open and brave as they are.

A Doubly Single Man

Fashion designer Tom Ford's directorial debut of Christopher Isherwood's novel *A Single Man* is a faithful yet artistic adaptation, and ultimately an extraordinary film. Financed by Ford himself, this stylistic work of art affords Colin Firth the role of a lifetime.

Set in Los Angeles on November 30, 1962, *A Single Man* is the story of George Falconer (Colin Firth), a middle-aged British college professor who has struggled to find meaning in his life since the sudden death eight months earlier of his longtime partner, Jim (Matthew Goode). Throughout the single day depicted in the film, and narrated from his point of view, George dwells on his past and his seemingly empty future as he prepares for his planned suicide that evening. Before meeting his close friend Charley (Julianne Moore) for dinner, he has unexpected encounters with a Spanish prostitute (Jon Kortajarena) and a young student, Kenny Potter (Nicholas Hoult), who has become fixated on George as a kindred spirit.

You'd expect a designer like Ford to make pretty pictures of pretty people wearing pretty clothes standing in pretty places, but unlike so many music video directors who are unable to combine beautifully shot images and symbols into narrative, Ford integrates style and substance in brilliant, effective, and evocative ways.

A Single Man is about, among other things, being single, and as

I watched the frames unspool and bathe the enormous screen, I began
to think about what this means. In one sense, we're all single. In another,
none of us are. When most people think of being single, they think of
someone who has no sexual partner, no primary person, no automatic
plus-one for every situation that calls for it. Of course, many, if not
most, still equate this with marriage. One is single until one is married.
But there are plenty of single married people; plenty of people who are
not married and couldn't be less single.

Interestingly, George doesn't just appear to be single now that
Jim is dead, but because their relationship is rejected by society, he
appeared to be so even when Jim was alive and they were together. This
is true of all secret or non-sanctioned relationships—which, at various
times and in various places, have included race, religion, sex, age, family,
nationality, number of partners, sexual orientation, etc.

George is an acutely single man in the sense that he isn't
allowed to truly grieve for his great love because family and friends
and coworkers and the community don't recognize the relationship,
don't value Jim and George and what they have. This imposes an
intolerable level of suffering atop an already unimaginable experience
of loss—a depth of isolation to join the desolation—that makes him a
doubly single man. Just imagine how this compounds and complicates,
extends and exponentially multiplies the difficulty of something that is
impossibly painful to begin with.

The book and the film include a fascinating discussion about
minorities and the fear they elicit from the majority. This fear is based
on a perceived threat, and whether it's because of race or religion or
sex or sexual orientation, it is the result of small-heartedness within the
haters that cause them to operate in fear and not love, inside a paradigm
of scarcity where the freedom, happiness, lifestyle, and even existence
of "the other" is seen as somehow robbing them of these very things.

Most of us, comfortably ensconced in the majority, can't
imagine what it's like to be a minority, but we should continually try.
And like Gregory Peck in *Gentleman's Agreement*, we should look for
opportunities to be a minority—or at least be thought of as a minority.
When we are empathetic, we are our very best selves. When we are
compassionate, we are most like God.

Because I have so many good, dear friends who happen to be
gay, and because I love and spend time with them—including in gay
friendly places and events, I've had people ask if I'm gay. This is a great

honor to me. And to all the homophobes out there (because it only matters to you), please consider me gay—in fact, consider me the gayest of gays.

In the midst of writing this, I took a lunch break at a restaurant showing the "don't ask, don't tell" hearings, and it struck me just how short a distance we've come in the forty-eight years since the events of *A Single Man*. How can we continue to justify our bigotry, our fear, our so very small minds, our utter lack of love? How can we continue to fashion all-too-human gods who lend a sense of righteousness to our prejudices?

The film takes place in the shadow of the Cuban Missile Crisis, and an already-dead-and-doesn't-know-it coworker tells George he should build a bomb shelter but not tell anyone, because, when it's needed, the world at that time won't be a place for sentiment. George, who knows more about death and loss and loneliness than his coworker could ever imagine, responds that he wouldn't want to live in such a world.

As a single man, George, like the rest of us, longs to make a meaningful connection with others—something he did with Jim, something his enormous grief makes impossible now. When one of his students observes how we're all trapped in the prisons of our own bodies and how we can never know what others are really like inside, never experience the world as they do, George recalls how the times he's spent connecting with other human beings have made his life worth living. Now, unable to connect, he no longer wants to live.

Throughout *A Single Man*, George talks about certain moments of clarity he experiences, and how they change him and transform his perspective, his very worldview, in ways he can scarcely describe. These revelations, these sublime epiphanies, are little reverberations of mystical insight, grace-filled glimpses that point to so much more—the more of life, the more that it and we can be. Watching *A Single Man* was just such an experience for me—a moving, memorable one of clarity, insight, even epiphany.

If You Have a Good
Appetite for Great Food and Film

On the drive to the theater to see *Julie & Julia*, I was thinking about a report I'd read earlier in the day about the rise of obesity in America—how two-thirds of us are either overweight or obese, and how on average we're twenty-three pounds overweight.

That was on the drive over. During and following the film, all I wanted to do was eat.

Of course, what I longed for was not what is making us fat—not poorly produced, corn-fed, high fructose corn syrup, calorie-and fat-injected food, but a fine meal—the kind that feeds the soul while nourishing the body.

What I settled on was three-quarters of an exquisite piece of key lime pie at Gracie Rae's, which did feed my soul, but not as much as the late-evening ambience, the sun-streaked bay, and the gentle kiss of evening on the soft, brine-tinged breeze.

The article I had read about how we're eating ourselves to death argued that obesity, like tobacco and alcohol abuse, isn't just dangerous, but expensive. New research shows medical spending averages $1,400 more a year for an obese person and the overall obesity-related health spending is around $147 billion, double what it was nearly a decade ago (according to the journal *Health Affairs*).

We've got a problem. Our approach to food. Our approach to life. The hole in the secret depths of who we are can't be filled with food alone.

Our great national sins, the ones so deeply a part of who we are they don't get very many sermons, don't get marches or signs or bumper stickers, and don't decide elections, are greed and gluttony. But this film is the antithesis of our self-destructive behavior—a celebration of good food and of women and marriage and life.

The film is about the appreciation, not the aberration and exploitation, of food. The way alcohol is not an issue for people who drink moderately, food is not an issue for non gluttons.

Food, like sex or work or religion or family or alcohol, can be both cause for and used in celebration—something that leads us into transcendence—or it can be merely something we do, mundane, thoughtless, animalistic.

For both Julia and Julie, food is far, far more than just fuel.

Julia Child (Meryl Streep) and Julie Powell (Amy Adams) are featured in writer-director Nora Ephron's adaptation of two bestselling memoirs, Powell's *Julie & Julia* and *My Life in France*, by Julia Child with Alex Prud'homme. Based on two true stories, *Julie & Julia* intertwines the lives of two women who, though separated by time and space, are both at loose ends—until they discover that with the right combination of passion, fearlessness, and butter, anything is possible.

We live in a time and a place of plenty, which won't last—it can't—but what do we do while it does? Can we have the discipline to deny ourselves, the compassion to share our undeserved abundance, the wisdom and humility to be grateful, the spiritual insight to perceive what is beyond nutritional necessity? The answers are all too obvious, but we're a young species. Maybe we'll survive our adolescence to become who we're meant to be.

We all have a relationship with food, and we all have to figure it out.

But food isn't the only relationship that is explored in the film. There's also Julie and Julia's relationships with friends and family and society, and especially their relationships with their husbands.

Both Julie and Julia became who they did thanks in part to the encouraging, supportive spouses in their lives. Rarely has marriage been so positively portrayed on-screen. Not only does Ms. Ephron love good food, but, after a very public unhappy marriage and acrimonious divorce, she now loves being married. Both her relationship to food and her husband shine through her script and her camera and onto the screen.

Julie & Julia teaches ever so gently that the keys to a good life and relationship are genuine love, respect, and support given to and received from our significant others, authenticity, real purpose, fidelity to self and calling, hard work, good food, good sex—and a good appetite for all of these.

Like a consummate chef preparing a special meal for treasured friends and family, Ms. Ephron has taken the recipes found in both Julie's and Julia's books, added her own ingredients, and cooked up a near flawless film. All that's left to say is bon appétit. Come with a good appetite to this good film about good people and good times and the good food that makes everything even better.

The Art of Dying

Synecdoche, New York is such a devastating, profound, and true masterwork of art I feel unequal to the task of telling you just how extraordinary, rare, stunning, and heartbreaking it really is.

Just prior to watching *Synecdoche, New York*, I was celebrating the brilliance of Charlie Kaufman, proclaiming *Eternal Sunshine of the Spotless Mind* to be the brightest object in his creative constellation. Now, after having seen *Synecdoche, New York*, I'm saying that what *Eternal Sunshine of the Spotless Mind* does for love and memory, *Synecdoche, New York* does for virtually everything else—most notably life, art, meaning, aging, dying, and death.

The thing about life is, we die. That's it. What does it mean to be human, but that we will one day be no more, and we are aware of it—some of us quite acutely.

When the film's protagonist, Caden Cotard, tells his cast and crew about the new play he wants to stage, he says, "I've been thinking a lot about death lately. That's what I want to explore. We're all hurtling toward death, yet here we are for a moment alive, each of us knowing we're gonna die, each of us secretly believing we won't."

Claire Keen, one of the female actors, responds, "That's brilliant... It's everything."

And though she says it out of a worshipful infatuation with

Caden, it's no less true.

More than any other film I can recall, *Synecdoche, New York* is so rich and multi-layered, its deepest profundity in the subtext, that it seems silly to try to tell what it's about, but here goes:

Theater director Caden Cotard is mounting a new play. Having won a MacArthur grant, he is determined to create a piece of brutal realism, something he can put his whole self into. He gathers an ensemble cast into a warehouse in Manhattan's theater district and directs them in a celebration of the mundane, instructing each to live out their constructed lives in a small mockup of the city outside. As the city inside the warehouse grows, Caden's own life veers wildly off the tracks. Populating the cast and crew with doppelgangers, he continually blurs the line between the world of the play and that of his own deteriorating reality.

The title is a play on Schenectady, New York, where part of the film is set. *Synecdoche* (pronounced si-NEK-duh-kee), from a Greek word meaning "simultaneous understanding," is a figure of speech in which a term denoting a part of something is used to refer to the whole thing. In the film, the play represents life, and so a part of life represents the whole of life and the New York within the play represents the New York outside the warehouse where it's being staged.

Does life imitate art? Do we each have doppelgangers wandering around, unseen by us, unknown to us, or, are we all one another's double—interchangeable in ways we can't even fathom because of our shared humanity and futility, in that we are alive and soon won't be? And like Caden's characters, women are interchangeable with men and vise versa (very Jungian anima/animus), because what we have in common—our mortality—makes us far more alike than not. In Caden's play, "All the world's a stage, And all the men and women merely players; They have their exits and their entrances, And one man in his time plays many parts."

Even as *Synecdoche, New York* is full of people interacting—some of them intimately—and even though there are doubles and doppelgangers, ultimately, like us, Caden is alone. In addition to everything else, the film, the play within the film, and Caden's journey, are about loneliness. The characters of the film, the actors in the play—even as they connect and share and become one another—are, like you and me, ultimately utterly alone.

Just two days after experiencing Caden's utter aloneness, I found myself alone at a funeral. Over the years, I've attended and spoken at a lot of funerals, but this was the only one I ever recall going to and sitting at alone, and as I sat there alone thinking about the birth, life, and death of the person who was alone in the box before me, I couldn't help but think of Caden, couldn't help but feel profoundly alone. And yet, having shared Caden's journey made me less alone somehow—or perhaps made my aloneness more bearable.

Synecdoche, New York must be watched multiple times. When you finish it the first time, start it over and watch it again. But even with numerous viewings, we won't understand everything in the film—and we're not meant to. Life is mysterious. Art that reflects it, the very kind of brutally truthful art Caden is trying to make, will be mysterious, will be, in many ways, incomprehensible. In life, in art, in religion, there aren't merely vague unknowns, but specific unknowables.

Though I think artists will likely relate to Caden most, there's plenty in his journey for everyone—for it's our journey, the betrayal of us by of our bodies, loss, regret, unrecognized potential, what is never quite living up to what might have been, sickness, suffering, aging, dying, and death.

Perhaps the word *genius* is tossed around too indiscriminately these days, but it fits here. Charlie Kaufman is truly a genius. His work requires us to work and then rewards us greatly for it. *Synecdoche, New York* isn't just a great film, it's perhaps one of the greatest films ever made. Like life, *Synecdoche, New York* is heartbreaking and painful, some parts particularly difficult to watch. It's not an easy film, not easy at all, but it's a worthy film—worth every moment invested into it. How many movies can you say that about?

Perhaps the greatest compliment I can give this matchless masterpiece of a play within a film is that it evokes within me echoes of the world's greatest playwright, particularly these haunting, desolate, immortal words that now seem to have been written for Caden Cotard: "All our yesterdays have lighted fools; The way to dusty death. Out, out, brief candle! Life's but a walking shadow, a poor player; That struts and frets his hour upon the stage; And then is heard no more: it is a tale; Told by an idiot, full of sound and fury, Signifying nothing."

Of course, that such words can be written, that such tales can be told argues against the very notion of nothingness it expresses to signify something. Quite something. And that's not nothing. In fact, it just might be everything.

In and Out

As I write this, I'm watching the Academy Awards, searching for inspiration, hoping something said in an acceptance speech or a scene played from last year's most-honored films will spark an idea.

And it worked.

But not like I imagined (imagine that).

Several ideas came. And went. Like falling flakes in too-warm weather, nothing stuck.

At one point, a friend IM'd me on Facebook and asked what I was doing. When I told her, she began to offer suggestions for what I might write about—most of them far better than my own thoughts. But, again, not one of the many wonderful seeds she was sowing took root.

And so, with a deadline looming, which of course they always do, I had many, many ideas, but not one that felt right.

Until…

I began to muse about the differences between ideas and inspiration.

I have ideas all the time—lots and lots of them; many before I ever started watching the Oscars—ideas for columns, novels, movies, short stories, and a host of other random and unrelated things. But in the way only one of the thousands of acorns that rain down from an enormous oak becomes itself an oak, few ideas are ever more than that—ideas.

Ideas are easy. Execution is the thing.

From the moment my first novel came out in the fall of 1997, I've had countless people want to give me their ideas for books—and my response is always the same. I can't get to all of my own ideas. And if it's your idea, it's probably your book to write.

Idea is defined as "a thought or conception, that potentially or actually exists in the mind as a product of mental activity; an opinion, conviction, or principle; a plan, scheme, or method; a notion; a fancy."

This isn't entirely unrelated to inspiration, but, in my experience, it's different enough to make all the difference in the world.

Inspiration is defined as "stimulation of the mind or emotions to a high level of feeling or activity; an agency that moves the intellect or emotions or prompts action or invention; a sudden creative act or idea, that is inspired; divine guidance or influence exerted directly on the mind and soul of humankind; the act of drawing in, especially the inhalation of air into the lungs."

These definitions get at part of what I think is the biggest difference between an idea and inspiration.

An idea remains a thought or concept in the mind, while inspiration stimulates us beyond thought and feeling into activity. Ideas are involved, of course.

Everything begins with an image, a thought, an idea—but, if inspiration, this is truly just the beginning. An idea can be a seed for inspiration, but inspiration moves us beyond the idea—the seed sprouts.

There's an alchemical process involving passion, maybe even obsession, that transforms an idea into an action or causes some ideas to be inspired, while others aren't (or aren't yet), and I no more understand it than any of the great, thrilling, humbling, inspiring mysteries of existence. But it is inspiring—inspiration itself inspires.

We can ponder ideas, but inspiration propels.

And though inspiration is a mystery—utterly beyond us and out of our control, we can court it.

I pursue and woo my muse with an earnest relentlessness akin to madness of a sort only certain types of obsessed lovers can fathom—spending my mornings and midnights trying to seduce her.

I fill my life with people and things I find inspirational—art and artists; books and writers; music, fun, friends; soulful sinners and saints, lovers, thinkers, characters; and kind, compassionate people.

My writing room, the space I spend more time in than any other, is filled with thousands and thousands of books, with photographs and paintings, with images and icons, with gifts and mementos. Often, particularly when I'm writing, the room flickers in candlelight, as incense and instrumental music float around.

But none of this guarantees inspiration. It's just preparation and invitation—invocation of a type not unlike religious devotion.

I never know what will inspire a column. Sometimes something in a mediocre movie will provoke a thought that blossoms, while a fine film or book, though inspiring in itself, offers me no way in, no tunnels, no hooks, nothing that sticks to grey cells, nothing that penetrates the soil of soul.

The same applies to all my creative endeavors—from novels to nature photography—and to nearly all of life.

If I don't know when or from where inspiration will come, I can but be ready at all times. I'm not, of course, but I attempt to be prepared, to be open, to look and listen, to seek and woo.

In this way, the writing life, like the creative life, like the soulful life, is like the best and wisest life any of us can lead. Hone our sensitivity and receptivity, be diligent in our preparation and searching, learn to listen, learn to live the Buddha's awakened life, for we never know when the still, small voice inside us will speak, when our muse will tickle our ear with soft whispers, when the wind or a wren might have a message for us.

As Frederick Buechner so extraordinarily and eloquently puts it, "Listen to your life. See it for the fathomless mystery that it is. In the boredom and pain of it no less than in the excitement and gladness: touch, taste, smell your way to the holy and hidden heart of it because in the last analysis all moments are key moments, and life itself is grace."

Ultimately, inspiration is a mystery, but it's as basic to our nature as breathing (the very act the word comes from)—drawing in and letting out. In and out. In and out. Just breathe. Breathe in the universe in each inspiring inhalation. This is meditation. This is inspiration. This is love. This is life. In and out. In and out. Removing any obstruction, all impediments, we open our hearts and minds, our souls and spirits, to the Mystery. In and out. In and out.

Acknowledgements

For support and encouragement and invaluable contributions:

Jim Pascoe, Adam Ake, Jennifer Jones, Lynn Wallace, Jill Mueller, Bette Powell, Fran Oppenheimer, Amy Moore-Benson, Jason Hedden, Emily Balazs, Ben Leroy, Michael Connelly, Mike and Judi Lister, Tony Simmons, Jeff Moore, Dave Lloyd, David Vest, Jan Waddy, Will Glover, Pam and Micah and Meleah Lister, Travis Roberson, and Harley Walsh.

Michael Lister

A native Floridian, award-winning novelist, Michael Lister grew up in North Florida near the Gulf of Mexico and the Apalachicola River where most of his books are set.

In the early 90s, Lister became the youngest chaplain within the Florida Department of Corrections—a unique experience that led to his critically acclaimed mystery series featuring prison chaplain John Jordan: POWER IN THE BLOOD, BLOOD OF THE LAMB, FLESH AND BLOOD, THE BODY AND THE BLOOD, and BLOOD SACRIFICE.

Michael won a Florida Book Award for his literary thriller, DOU-BLE EXPOSURE, a book, according to the *Panama City News Herald*, that "is lyrical and literary, written in a sparse but evocative prose reminiscent of Cormac McCarthy." His other novles include THUNDER BEACH, THE BIG GOODBYE, BUNRT OFFERINGS, and SEPARATION ANXI-ETY.

Michael's next book is a meditation on how to have the best life possible titled, LIVING IN THE HOT NOW.

His website is www.MichaelLister.com.

FINDING THE WAY AGAIN

Rediscovering Radical Love and Freedom in the Lost Teachings of Jesus

author of *The Body and the Blood*

Michael Lister

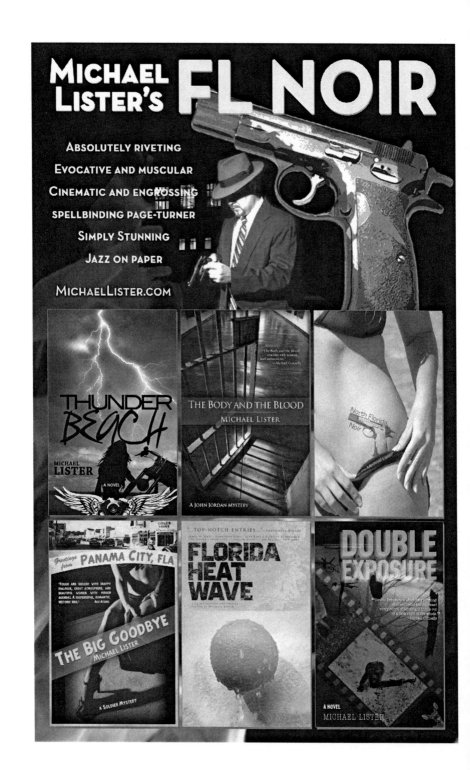

MICHAEL LISTER's FL NOIR

ABSOLUTELY RIVETING

EVOCATIVE AND MUSCULAR

CINEMATIC AND ENGROSSING

SPELLBINDING PAGE-TURNER

SIMPLY STUNNING

JAZZ ON PAPER

MICHAELLISTER.COM

THUNDER BEACH
MICHAEL LISTER
A NOVEL

THE BODY AND THE BLOOD
MICHAEL LISTER
"The Body and the Blood crackles with tension and authenticity."
—Michael Connelly
A JOHN JORDAN MYSTERY

North Florida Noir

Greetings from PANAMA CITY, FLA
"Tough and violent with snappy dialogue, great atmosphere, and beautiful women with hidden agendas. A suspenseful, romantic, historic ride."
Ace Atkins
THE BIG GOODBYE
MICHAEL LISTER
A SOLDIER MYSTERY

TOP-NOTCH ENTRIES
FLORIDA HEAT WAVE
EDITED BY MICHAEL LISTER

DOUBLE EXPOSURE
A NOVEL
MICHAEL LISTER

You buy a book.

Chapter 7

Pulpwood Press

Where Books of Life become Trees of Life become Books of Life

We plant a tree.

CPSIA information can be obtained at www.ICGtesting.com
Printed in the USA
LVOW120730020212

266549LV00001B/2/P